How we made it in Africa

How we made it in Africa

Learn from the stories of 25 entrepreneurs who've built thriving businesses

Compiled by Jaco Maritz

MARITZ AFRICA
CAPE TOWN

Published by Maritz Africa

Unit 205, The Hills, Buchanan Square
154 Sir Lowry Road
Woodstock
Cape Town
South Africa
7925

www.maritzafrica.com

How we made it in Africa: Learn from the stories of 25 entrepreneurs who've built thriving businesses
Print edition ISBN 978-0-6208184-3-8

Editor: Jaco Maritz
Copy editor: Erla Rabe
Proofreaders: Melissa Cawthra, Margy Beves-Gibson
Cover design: Fuel Design
Printed by Print on Demand, Cape Town, South Africa

DISCLAIMER

Contents

Our Sponsors

The publisher would like to thank the University of Cape Town Graduate School of Business and BUSINESS/PARTNERS for their support in making this publication a reality.

UNIVERSITY OF CAPE TOWN GRADUATE SCHOOL OF BUSINESS

The University of Cape Town Graduate School of Business (GSB) is internationally renowned as one of a handful of business schools in Africa with the prestigious triple-crown accreditation with endorsements from EQUIS (the European Foundation for Management Development), AACSB (The Association to Advance Collegiate Schools of Business), and AMBA (The Association of MBAs).

As a top school with more than five decades of experience in the emerging market, the GSB has a responsibility to engage with its socio-political and economic context. Its teaching, learning and research are directed towards building a more economically prosperous, more equitable, and more integrated continent. The school is constantly investing in quality scholarship and strong partnerships to support these aims through initiatives like the Allan Gray Centre for Values-Based Leadership, the Bertha Centre for Social Innovation and Entrepreneurship, the Raymond Ackerman Academy of Entrepreneurial Development, and the MTN Solution Space.

Our top-ranked academic programmes are structured to refine professional knowledge, enhance leadership ability and give individuals the skills and confidence needed to grow innovative new ideas into financially sound, long-term development solutions.

www.gsb.uct.ac.za/course-finder

BUSINESS/PARTNERS

BUSINESS/PARTNERS is a specialist risk finance company that provides customised financial solutions, technical assistance and mentorship, sectoral knowledge, business premises and other value-added services for formal small and medium enterprises (SMEs) in South Africa and selected African countries, namely Kenya, Malawi, Namibia, Rwanda, Uganda and Zambia. As of March 2018, the company had invested R18.5 billion in SMEs since inception in 1981.

We pride ourselves as being the home of the entrepreneur. We're passionate about funding, supporting and mentoring entrepreneurs, or as we like to call them, the "square pegs in a sea of round holes" because they are the exceptional individuals who see the world not for what it is, but for what it could be.

Entrepreneurs almost always work against the grain, often challenging conformity, because they see the world through fresh eyes. Where others see problems and challenges, they see opportunities and turn them into solutions. They share an unwavering belief in their abilities and skills to solve problems while fulfilling societal needs. Statistics show that only one in a handful of people possesses the qualities to be an entrepreneur. They are truly special.

www.businesspartners.co.za

Our Early Supporters

Special thank you to the following individuals and companies for supporting this project during its early stages.

Chad Pennington (Sobitart Photography)
Amit Gadhia (Gadhia Law, Nairobi)
Ayaan Chitty (HR Tech Africa)
Marylyn Manyange (Kanzungu.Inc)
Salum Awadh (SSC Holdings)
Enviu
Francois B. Arthanas (FRICASHOP.COM)
Phila Dlamini
Cleopatra Douglas
Ickmar Balyn

Preface

"Sir, sir," called the young man sitting by himself next to the road in the dusty and remote northern Nigerian city of Sokoto. He was fiddling with a car engine using battered tools scattered on a flimsy wooden table.

"I'm an engineer," he proclaimed proudly, much to my surprise. "How can I help you?"

Because of his modest set-up and the fact that there weren't any other merchants around him, I initially didn't label him an entrepreneur. But I was wrong – this was his workshop and he was ready to do business.

I was in town for only a few days and unfortunately didn't have any machinery for him to fix. But, a decade later, the scene still sticks with me. It is a classic example of the entrepreneurial spirit and hustling mentality for which Nigerians are well known.

In this book, we tell the stories of 25 entrepreneurs from across Africa who've built thriving businesses. While many of them now run multi-million-dollar ventures, they started out with the same can-do attitude as the budding engineer.

Over the years, *How we made it in Africa*, the award-winning pan-African online business magazine I founded in 2010, has profiled hundreds of the continent's most interesting entrepreneurs. For this book, we caught up with some of those we've written about in the past, and interviewed others for the first time. The longer book format provided space to delve much deeper into how these businesspeople built their companies than what the economics of online publishing allows for.

We deliberately didn't profile some of Africa's more well-known business personalities (such as Nigerian cement tycoon Aliko Dangote, Zimbabwean telecoms pioneer Strive Masiyiwa or South African mining magnate Patrice Motsepe), instead introducing some fresh names, with a particular focus on the next generation, which in the coming decades could very well be mentioned alongside these titans.

Our aim is for readers to learn from, and be inspired by, the experiences of Africa's most dynamic entrepreneurs, while simultaneously gaining insight into the continent's business opportunities. Each entrepreneur's story is written in an honest and sober manner, not shying away from the mistakes made and the considerable hurdles they had to overcome.

As an entrepreneur myself, I know that running your own business is an intense rollercoaster ride, where the highs are high, and the lows debilitatingly low. From finding investors and making that first sale, to managing difficult employees and dealing with cash flow crises, the book offers real-life examples of coping with the challenges of the business world.

Nelly Tuikong, founder of Kenyan beauty brand Pauline Cosmetics, best captures the spirit of the book: "Business is sweet and sour. It is the most frustrating thing you will ever do. I tend to keep my emotions under control because it is how I was raised. So when my husband sees me crying, he knows things are really bad. There are times when I need to do just that – cry, binge on some TV shows, eat a whole tub of ice cream. But then I pull myself up again the next day. It is very frustrating, but it is one of the most incredible journeys you will ever take."

This book is also not exclusively aimed at businesspeople but for anyone who wants to make the most of their limited time on Earth; for those who want to see their dreams and ambitions, whatever they are, become a reality. As Dr Hend El Sherbini, CEO of Egyptian healthcare company IDH, says: the definition of success is simply to accomplish what you really want to achieve.

We hope you find this book an interesting and enriching read.

Jaco Maritz
14 October 2018

1.

Ken Njoroge

The long, hard journey to build a billion-dollar company

By Jaco Maritz & Justin Probyn

When starting out, most entrepreneurs typically have a rough idea of where they want to take their companies. But as they are confronted with real-world realities such as a lack of money, increasing competition, staff matters and changing market forces, the bigger goal often starts taking a back seat in the battle for survival. Vision and mission statements can quickly become little more than PR tools and words on the company website.

Ken Njoroge, the Kenyan co-founder and co-CEO of pan-African digital payments business Cellulant, is someone for whom the original vision remains front and centre of every-thing the company does, even more than 15 years after starting the business. In fact, he and Bolaji Akinboro, his Nigerian part-ner and co-CEO, decided on a goal before they were even a hundred per cent certain of the type of business through which it would be accomplished.

Their goal? To build a $1-billion company. They didn't pick this figure because they were "particularly interested in driving Ferraris". It symbolised something bigger. It was to dispel the myth that "Africans can't do anything for themselves" and demonstrate that it is possible to build a world-class company without political connections or paying bribes.

"Our stories and how we grew up, are very similar," says Njoroge. "After we became friends, we spent a lot of time complaining about the state of things in Africa. Everywhere in the world we looked, we saw Africans doing great things in multinational corporations. Then we looked at the state of our own continent and had to ask: What's wrong with us? That's when we decided to do something about it," Njoroge tells.

But why specifically $1 billion and not $100 million, or even $10 million, which would be equally respectable?

Because $10 million is not enough for Njoroge, who says that a friend of a corrupt politician could relatively easily accumulate this much. Even $100 million can be achieved by a "couple of guys who stole oil money in Angola or Nigeria". But a $1-billion company requires a top-notch operation. "At that size, no one can have an excuse for being mediocre in Africa. That was our motivation – it is the thing that drives us."

Njoroge says it is crucial that entrepreneurs take the time to formulate the *why* of their business, as it will drive all their decisions, from who to employ to what processes to put in place.

CUTTING HIS TEETH

Njoroge calls the first time he connected to the internet "a very powerful experience". "I was like a kid in a candy store. I love reading and with the internet I could find information on any topic and read a bunch of things that took me in any direction."

Inspired by the likes of Yahoo and Netscape, he began to see the business opportunities the internet offered. He was drawn to the possibility of building a "knowledge business" from anywhere in the world using only "what's in your head".

After obtaining a graduate diploma in information systems management from Nairobi's Strathmore University, Njoroge worked at a handful of internet service providers (ISPs) at a time when the internet was a relatively new concept in Kenya.

Then, in 1998, he founded his first company, a web-development firm called 3mice, with two partners. The name was a play on a computer mouse and the company having three founders. "The name turned out to be one of the best branding decisions we made. People joked about it, but they never forgot it," recalls Njoroge.

The start-up worked from a "small, dirty kitchen" in an upmarket Nairobi suburb. "When someone asked where our office was, I'd say, 'It is in a cool area.' And it was – the dirty kitchen was in a cool area," says Njoroge. Luckily clients rarely visited their office.

With relatively few competitors in the market at the time, 3mice signed several blue-chip companies, such as East African Breweries, Safaricom and Coca-Cola. They built one of the first big e-commerce websites in the region for Virtual City, developed an online booking platform for Kenya Airways and worked on a Uganda Securities Exchange project.

Njoroge became increasingly interested in the mobile telecoms industry which, although in its infancy, was growing rapidly. To explore opportunities in the sector, he formed a separate research and development team at 3mice, called The Mobile Project. "We spent a lot of time engaging with 3mice's mobile-operator customers to figure out where the industry was headed," he says.

It was during this time that Njoroge met Bolaji Akinboro,

who was in Kenya to work on a World Bank-initiated project to create an open and affordable distance-learning institution for the continent, called African Virtual University. They clicked immediately and spent hours discussing business and a host of other topics of mutual interest.

At 3mice, the partners eventually decided to go their own ways. It was agreed that Njoroge would give back his shares in the company in return for The Mobile Project that had one retainer client and a handful of staff. In 2002, he registered a stand-alone entity, called Cellulant, with Akinboro as his co-founder.

MAKING MONEY FROM MOBILE RINGTONES

Cellulant initially concentrated on selling mobile ringtones and music. They charged around $1 a track and customers paid using their prepaid mobile airtime.

Akinboro wasn't active in the day-to-day operations and continued to work full-time for two reasons. Firstly, they boot-strapped the business and had little money, which meant one of them had to earn a salary. Secondly, they thought it would be good for the company's governance to have "one guy sitting on the outside asking hard questions". Njoroge took on the role of CEO.

Although Cellulant was based in Kenya, their first ringtone services were launched in Uganda and Ghana where they part-nered with mobile operators. Unfortunately, there wasn't much money in it and on top of that, Njoroge frequently had to "scrape together coins" for flights to be able to keep an eye on the businesses. "We looked at each other and said, 'We are Kenyan and Nigerian – what are we doing in Uganda and Ghana when we are barely making ends meet?'" That was when they decided to focus their efforts on Kenya and Nigeria, where the markets were much bigger, too.

It turned out it was less easy to gain entry into their home countries than it was in Uganda and Ghana. Cellulant spent a long time negotiating with mobile operators and regulatory bodies to get their service up and running. "In Kenya there was literally no regulatory framework for what we were doing. The copyright frameworks did not exist and things took three times longer than we thought they would."

After much back and forth they eventually launched on Kenya's Celtel (now Airtel) and Safaricom networks in 2004. That same year they also rolled out an offering in Nigeria.

Cellulant needed good employees, but as Njoroge didn't have much financial resources to work with, he hired "diamonds in the rough who just needed some polishing" – inexperienced employees eager to learn and willing to commit for the long term. He is not convinced that highly experienced people are always the best fit for a start-up environment and therefore "got people who had a lot of potential, who had a lot of fight in them, but hadn't realised it yet".

The first few years in business were tough. Njoroge describes it as "a series of near-death experiences". Many months they did not have money to pay salaries, which meant employees couldn't meet their financial commitments either. Njoroge says he'll never forget the day his chief technology officer (CTO) didn't turn up for work because he had trouble with his landlord as he hadn't paid his rent. "I knew if I didn't get our CTO's mind back to his work, we wouldn't complete our projects on time, which would mean that we wouldn't get paid and would damage our reputation. So I said to him, 'You get back to work, let me talk to your landlord.'"

Njoroge married within a year of starting Cellulant and the company's struggles had a big toll on his personal life. "There was no salary in the business for me. With whatever little money there was, I paid the employees first. The business always came first. If a client gave us a cheque and I had to buy a computer server, I would buy the server instead of paying my rent. Of course my family suffered." Many times there wasn't even money for diapers for his newborn baby. "Those were very tough times. I sold every asset I could. I borrowed money from everybody I could. If you ask me how I did it, I honestly don't know."

Not even the prospect of much-needed money from an outside source could turn Njoroge's attention away from Cellulant and their vision of building a $1-billion business. During this desperate period a company offered him a freelance assignment to develop a web strategy. Even though the fee was €4 000 ($4 600), and although he had gained considerable expertise in this field during his 3mice days, he turned down the job.

"I knew that €4 000 would be like a cocaine shot. Once I had it, I'd want another and then another – before I knew it, I wouldn't be focusing on Cellulant anymore. So that discussion did not go past a phone call."

But Njoroge persevered and the business gradually built up momentum. By 2006, the company was in a relatively stable position. "It was a very slow and tough start, but through persistence and resilience we convinced operators and musicians to come to the table and began to build fairly steady revenues."

CHANGING COURSE

With Cellulant out of crisis mode, the co-founders had time to reflect on its future and how they were tracking their $1-billion goal. They asked themselves: "Are we going to become a billion-dollar company by selling music?" It was clear that they weren't. "Music was a good business, but we needed to think of something that could become bigger."

They began exploring mobile payments platforms, which would also allow them to get a bigger slice of the music business revenue. Up until then, their customers were paying with prepaid airtime, which made Cellulant reliant on mobile network operators. For every $1 song Cellulant sold, the operator typically took about 80 per cent, leaving them with 20 cents. It therefore made sense to build a payment platform that would allow customers to pay Cellulant directly from their bank accounts and bypass the network operators.

The trigger to pivot into a new direction came in 2006 when Safaricom launched its free music service. Almost overnight, Cellulant's business declined by 70 per cent. Again, they couldn't pay salaries and were gasping for air.

"We decided that we couldn't have a business where our fundamental billing platform depended on somebody else's goodwill. Our music business was too dependent on mobile operators. It was a good business, but it wasn't resilient enough," says Njoroge.

They approached all the big banks with a proposal for a mobile banking platform. But it was such a new concept that none of the banks were interested. For two years they couldn't convince a single one.

Then Safaricom launched another new product in 2007: the revolutionary mobile-money platform M-Pesa, which allows subscribers to transfer money between one another and deposit and withdraw cash through a network of agents.

Within a year, M-Pesa had over a million subscribers. Banks

saw M-Pesa as a threat and were scrambling to get onto the mobile-banking bandwagon. "They remembered us and said, 'Hang on, there are these guys in the corner of Nairobi called Cellulant who have been talking about this thing for a long time. Let's call them.' Fear of M-Pesa persuaded banks to pay attention to us. That is how we happened to be in the right place at the right time."

It is how Cellulant came to launch its first white-labelled mobile wallet which could run with or without internet connectivity in 2009. Very quickly almost all of Kenya's large banks, including Standard Chartered, Kenya Commercial Bank and Diamond Trust Bank, offered mobile banking solutions using Cellulant's software. The banks paid Cellulant a set-up fee, ongoing maintenance charges and Cellulant earned a percentage of each transaction.

As the banks expanded their mobile-banking services to other countries in Africa, they took Cellulant with them. "We built our country footprint by basically following multinational banks," notes Njoroge. Cellulant's services are currently available in 11 African countries. They have also launched their own branded digital payments platform called Mula, which allows users to pay their utility bills and buy airtime.

TRANSFORMING NIGERIA'S AGRICULTURAL SECTOR

One of Cellulant's most impactful endeavours is a digital platform used to distribute government subsidies to millions of Nigerian farmers since 2012. Previously, the Nigerian government had spent hundreds of millions of dollars to buy and distribute fertiliser and seed to small-scale farmers, but only about 11 per cent of the fertiliser reached the farmers. The bulk was stolen by the so-called fertiliser mafia.

Cellulant became involved after a chance meeting on a plane. In July 2011, Njoroge and the company's chairman, Samuel Kiruthu, were on a routine flight to Lagos, when they met Akinwumi Adesina, the then vice president of the Alliance for a Green Revolution in Africa (AGRA). They began discussing the problems riddling Nigeria's fertiliser subsidies and Adesina asked Njoroge how he would solve it. For the next three hours on the plane, the three hammered out a solution that involved an e-wallet and sending subsidies directly to the farmers.

"We painted such a compelling business case that Adesina looked at me and said: 'This is a very interesting discussion, I think I should introduce you to the Central Bank Governor.' Then he said, 'No, I think you should meet the President.'"

In a sheer stroke of luck, Adesina was shortly thereafter appointed Minister of Agriculture and Rural Development and four months later, after Njoroge's team had done some groundwork in Nigeria, they were invited to pitch their concept to a group of top government officials which included Adesina, the Minister of Finance, the Central Bank Governor and the Minister of Communication Technology. "At the end of a four-hour grilling, the Finance Minister said, 'Gentlemen, it is November. The rains come in February. If we make this our policy, there is no plan B. There is no turning back. We cannot delay the rain and the programme has to be live before it comes. All these nice things you guys have told us ... it better be on the ground,'" recalls Njoroge.

Njoroge and Akinboro left the meeting "somewhat in a daze". The government officials gave Cellulant a verbal yes but there was no contract in place and there wasn't time to get everything in black and white. "We had eight weeks to get the platform to market and decided to take a leap of faith," says Njoroge. They secured a bank loan of $500 000 and Akinboro, who was still working full-time for another company, put in leave to manage the project.

Njoroge knew it was going to be tough to write the software in a matter of weeks but he also knew that he had "built his entire career on completing projects in half the time others took". Cellulant assembled a team of 17 software developers in an apartment in Abuja, Nigeria's capital. "Teams were sleeping side by side on mattresses in one apartment. By then we had six weeks to get to market. It was an incredible journey. But we made it before the rain came – and we rolled out countrywide."

Cellulant's platform removed the state and the middlemen from the distribution of agricultural input subsidies. Farmers now register with the programme known as the Growth Enhancement Support Scheme (GESS) and receive digital vouchers on their mobile phones which entitles them to a 50 per cent discount – in other words, their subsidies – on fertiliser and seed at agri-dealers and distribution centres. Within three years, close to 15 million farmers had signed up with GESS.

With GESS as the foundation, Cellulant has been able to add to the services it offers with a marketplace that connects all the players in the agricultural value chain. Today, this platform, known as Agrikore, accounts for almost 60 per cent of Cellulant's business.

GETTING TO GRIPS WITH RUNNING A LARGE COMPANY

Cellulant has 350 full-time employees and Njoroge says managing a bigger team continues to be a steep learning curve for him.

He admits he was a tough boss when the company was still

fighting for survival. "We were essentially in a state of war and I was the general of a small army directing the war. I know people called me pushy and stubborn, and that I set unrealistic goals."

When the business reached 25 employees, his management style became untenable. Everyone was still reporting to Njoroge and he began causing bottlenecks. Njoroge sensed that all was not well and brought in a consultant to do a culture survey. The consultant presented his findings to the entire management team during a two-hour presentation that Njoroge describes as "really uncomfortable". In a nutshell, he found that Njoroge was the problem.

"The reason people weren't particularly happy was because of me: I made all the decisions, I didn't tell anybody what I was thinking, nobody understood why we were doing something a certain way, I was pushy, I didn't take any dissent, I didn't accept any feedback," Njoroge explains.

As a result, he worked on changing his style and began building the management team to take some of the responsibility off his shoulders. However, he says he is still learning. "It is a very long journey. I am a perfectionist and I want things done my way. Seeing something go wrong and having to resist the temptation to pick up the ball and run with it myself is not easy. I am not even sure that I have found a balance. I think parts of that report would still be relevant today."

What has changed is that, instead of ordering people around and pressuring them, he now "sells the vision" behind a project to the team leader and makes sure they feel a sense of ownership. Njoroge gives an example of when, in 2017, a pan-African bank appointed Cellulant to roll out a mobile-banking platform across 33 countries in four languages in 90 days.

Njoroge called a senior employee who he knew could run the project. He explained the ambitious scope of the work and said, "I'm going to call you back in an hour and then you can tell me whether it is a project you want to take on.

"I explain the intensity of a project and give the person the choice as to whether they want to run with it. In that way I have become more subtle." In the end, the person he called did accept the project and Cellulant delivered within 84 days.

In May 2018, Cellulant raised $47.5 million from a string of high-profile investors in one of the largest fintech deals in Africa. Njoroge believes that the company is well on its way to reach a valuation of $1 billion within the next seven years as long as it sustains its current growth rate.

"We knew that achieving our goal was going to be a very long journey, but if it is the only thing I did with my life, I'd be really happy," says Njoroge.

But when he now, at 43, thinks back to those early days when he couldn't pay his rent for five months or put food on the table or afford diapers for his baby, Njoroge says he can't see himself repeating the journey.

"Knowing what I know now, I wouldn't even dare."

2.

Tseday Asrat

A modern twist on Ethiopia's coffee culture

By Jeanette Clark

The founder and CEO of Kaldi's Coffee in Ethiopia starts her workday promptly at five every morning with a strong Americano. By this time, she has completed her daily paperwork and admin at her home office. When her day ends, strictly at 5pm, she has lost count of the number of macchiatos she has consumed.

Coffee is part of Tseday Asrat's life and it is her business.

Thousands of customers frequent the 38 Kaldi's cafés in Addis Ababa and Bishoftu in Ethiopia every day. The brand's instantly recognisable green and white circular logo features the outline of a traditional Ethiopian finjal cup full of steaming coffee next to a handful of coffee beans.

As an Ethiopian Airlines captain, her husband, Elias Ketema, has travelled extensively and loved the culture and style of coffee chains like Costa and Starbucks and brands such as Illy, Java and Lavazza. Tseday openly admits this has been the inspiration for the modern twist she brought to the way coffee is consumed in the country known as the birthplace of the roasted bean drink.

Had it not been for an insurmountable obstacle which caused

the demise of her first venture, Kaldi's might never have been. In 2003, Tseday was managing two thriving clothing boutiques and was set to become a successful Ethiopian fashion entrepreneur. Then, due to city planning and expansion, she was forced to vacate both premises: one, because the landlord wanted to demolish the building to build a bigger one, and the other because the city needed the land to construct a new road. "I was very angry and cried when I told my husband," Tseday says.

It was Elias who suggested moving into a completely new direction with a coffee café in the style of the modern, customer-focused brands he'd seen abroad. Tseday liked the idea but the rent for a spot in a prime location in Addis Ababa was prohibitive. The solution came in the form of a benefactor – a friend of Tseday and Elias – Sheikh Mohammed Hussein Al Amoudi, a millionaire businessman widely regarded as the largest private investor in Ethiopia.

Al Amoudi offered to cover the rent for Tseday's new venture for two years. Thereafter Kaldi's would have to be self-sustainable. No repayment was expected – it was a gift – and Tseday says she realises she was incredibly lucky to be given such a big break.

"I was lucky to have great people supporting and funding my business at the beginning, so it is important to me to give back now," she says. For every new branch that opens, Kaldi's selects one outstanding student from an underprivileged family in grade eight, the final year in primary school, and pays their fees and all other expenses at a private school. They have been doing this since 2013.

FROM MODELLING TO COFFEE AND BEYOND

Tseday grew up as the second of four children to civil servant parents in middle-class Ethiopia and says she was the rebel in the family: "I do things my way. My parents were often unhappy with the fact that I didn't take instruction from them, but when I believe in something, I have to do it. I will handle the consequences as they come."

When she was 17, she saw an advertisement by Elite Models, which was scouting for new talent in Addis Ababa. She went to the screening with a friend and all of a sudden Tseday was living the life of a successful commercial model with campaigns for companies like Coca-Cola and Philips. This did not sit well with her conservative parents. "They took so many disciplinary steps to try and stop me. They did not like the idea. I did it anyway," she says.

Tseday saved up her modelling fees and decided to open a fashion boutique in Addis Ababa. She credits her mother with planting the entrepreneurial seed in her. When she and her sisters were young, Ethiopian traders placed orders with her mother, who travelled to Dubai to buy the merchandise which they then bought from her. At the turn of the century, Tseday's mother – who by this time had seen the benefit and merit of her daughter's modelling career – lent her the rest of the money she needed to open her first boutique, Seasonal Style.

A year later, Tseday launched a second boutique and employed her sisters in the stores. The future looked bright – until she was told to vacate both premises at the same time.

Tseday was newly married and pregnant with her second child. It looked as if her hard work had come to a dead end. Al Amoudi's offer gave her a new lease on life.

In 2004, the first Kaldi's Coffee opened in Bole Street near the popular area that now houses Edna Mall in Addis Ababa. Tseday had sold the remaining merchandise from her boutiques and used the money to equip and decorate the café. The name Kaldi's acknowledges Kaldi, the Sufi goatherd who, legend has it, discovered the coffee plant in the ninth century in what is today Ethiopia, after seeing how energised his goats became after eating the red berries.

Finding a location and getting all the necessary approvals and permissions was a relatively smooth process. The first real challenge came when she had to manage staff. "In the boutiques I only had my sisters and one other lady. Suddenly I had to manage 32 people," she remembers.

Before that, she first had to find people who had the right skills, something that is an ongoing challenge. Ethiopian customers do not want to stand in a queue and order at a counter. They prefer to sit at a table and order from a waitron. "We have a long way to go before we'll be able to match our customer service with our customers' expectations. I had to learn how to serve a customer. I had to put on my uniform and be a waitress to learn what is expected," she says. Only then could she train her staff.

Ethiopians take their coffee seriously. A traditional coffee ceremony easily takes hours to complete. Kaldi's was not the first café to offer machine-brewed quick-service coffee, but Tseday believes it is the modern café atmosphere and decor that make it a success. "From the day we opened the first café, it was always full. Young people and young families like being there and having their coffee and ice cream. We served new items like iced coffee drinks and a variety of cakes that interested them," she says. These innovations paid off and helped to establish the Kaldi's brand in Ethiopia.

Additional branches were steadily added over the years, each funded by proceeds from the existing outlets. Tseday takes care every time in selecting the location – parking availability is particularly important, she says.

As they grew, it became increasingly difficult to maintain consistency in quality across the different outlets. Soon Kaldi's experienced challenges in their supply chain. Each café was sourcing milk from local dairy farmers but it was often watered down or of poor quality. They also obtained coffee from different suppliers, which meant the quality fluctuated. Customer complaints began to come in.

"Instead of giving up, I saw it as an opportunity to start our own supply company to assure Kaldi's of the quality and quantities it needs. It motivated me to do more and create more jobs," Tseday says. As a result, she diversified and added a dairy producer and milk-processing company, Loni Agro, as well as a roastery which buys coffee on the Ethiopian Commodity Exchange (ECX) to her business interests. Kaldi's has more than 1 800 employees with another 175 people employed at Loni Agro.

Apart from these businesses, which were added solely to overcome challenges in the supply chain, Tseday is also the co-owner of Gusto Italian restaurants in Addis Ababa. And in May 2018, the couple announced that FC Speciality Restaurant PLC, their company, is bringing KFC to Ethiopia with investments from RENEW Investment Advisory and Impact Angel Network. Their plan is to open the first KFC in 2018 and another seven in the next three years.

HOW BADLY DO YOU WANT IT?

In 2017, Kaldi's total sales in Ethiopia amounted to 155 million birr ($5.5 million) and they opened five new cafés in the last 12 months. Yet, good performance in the past is not a guarantee of lifelong success and Tseday knows she has to remain vigilant and focused to keep the business growing.

One challenge which persists is service quality and Tseday spends about 30 per cent of her time on training. The chain has established a dedicated training department, which incorporates leadership and mind-set training for all employees. The HR department's motto is "employment, training, promotion", in that order. "We usually contact the city and sub-city youth organisations when we are looking for new employees. They send us young people and we hire them without any experience, because our demand is high. Then we start their continuous on-the-job training. After years of experience and good evaluations, we then give opportunities for promotion to the existing internal staff," she says.

It is unusual for a CEO to spend this much time in the training department and Tseday concedes that it takes her away from her other management duties but believes it is critical. "I have to make sure that our employees see what I see and understand my vision for the company. I have to train them to do what I expect of them and inspect and monitor their work as often as needed."

A more recent headache is the devaluation of the Ethiopian birr that came into effect in October 2017 when the currency lost 15 per cent of its value. The National Bank of Ethiopia announced the move to address the country's foreign exchange shortage.

Although a lack of foreign exchange places pressure on her businesses as they import many of their raw materials, the devaluation immediately increased the cost of these materials. At the same time, the fact that Ethiopia has one of the fastest-growing economies in sub-Saharan Africa has brought complications of its own. The first Kaldi's store on Bole Street had to close in 2016 when the landlord did not renew their lease. The growth in some business sectors, specifically in the banking industry, caused a situation in the rental market where store owners often find that landlords simply won't renew their leases. The landlords favour long-term rental contracts with the banks, which are prepared to pay up-front for years in advance in order to secure the location. "They kicked me out," Tseday states.

"The most important question you have to ask yourself before doing something or starting something new is: 'How badly do I want it?' Your answer should not be because someone you know is doing this or that. It shouldn't be because your friends or family are telling you to start a business. You yourself should have the passion to pursue your dream. If you know how badly you want it, it will give you the mental toughness – it will give you the endurance. The bureaucracy or a shortage of foreign currency can never be the reason you did not chase your dream," she says.

3.

Tumi Phake

Flexing his entrepreneurial muscles to exploit a gap in the health club industry

By Justin Probyn & Jaco Maritz

In April 2014, a 30-year-old Tumi Phake clocked out from his job as a structured-lending specialist at Rand Merchant Bank (RMB) for the last time to start his own business. Despite having a degree in finance and spending seven years with RMB, it wasn't the financial sector that Phake had his sights on.

He had spotted a gap in the fitness industry and the very next month he founded Zenzele Fitness, which installs and manages fully equipped, in-house health clubs at large companies. Zenzele's clients typically provide the premises and indirectly subsidise the equipment and operational costs; this allows their staff to exercise for much less than they'd pay to belong to a commercial gym.

Despite leaving RMB, Phake draws inspiration from the three South African banking pioneers – Paul Harris, Laurie Dippenaar and GT Ferreira – who grew the bank from a modest initial investment back in 1977 to one of the cornerstones of the FirstRand financial services empire, which today also includes First National Bank, WesBank and Ashburton Investments. "Working at a corporate was very valuable and necessary, especially when it comes to understanding business governance. Yet I always knew at the back of my mind that I wanted to have my own company which I could grow and scale into at least a half-a-billion-rand business. That is my vision," Phake says. "If someone else, such as FirstRand, could do it, why can't I give it a shot?"

After he had handed in his resignation, a puzzled colleague commented, "You are going to run a gym? You've got such a great job."

"She thought I was a little crazy. It did make me doubt myself and I wondered if I wasn't making a big mistake, but I knew it could work," Phake says. "I've since learnt that when someone says something like that, they are just projecting their own fears. Looking back, my life is financially much better than it would have been if I'd stayed with the bank."

A NEW TAKE ON HEALTH CLUBS

South Africa already had a relatively well-developed health club industry, with Virgin Active and Planet Fitness as the prominent chains. Virgin Active, which controls at least 60 per cent of the market, was established in 2001 when Nelson Mandela reportedly asked Richard Branson to save thousands of jobs by taking over the liquidated Health and Racquet Club. In 2015, private equity firm Brait, in which well-known South African businessman Christo Wiese is a significant shareholder, bought an 80 per cent stake in Virgin Active.

Gyms are big business in South Africa but Phake, a fitness enthusiast himself, had something else in mind. His initial idea, which he had been nurturing for years, was to open gyms in lower-income neighbourhoods and outlying areas where mainstream health clubs did not go. Growing up in Tembisa, a township on the outskirts of Johannesburg, the only modern gyms he could find were in affluent suburbs. "I knew there was a need for gyms which would be accessible and affordable for everyone and thought that perhaps I could be the person to start one."

During his time at RMB, Phake used the office gym which gave him his first experience of a fitness centre in a corporate environment. Because it was partly subsidised by the bank, employees could work out for next to nothing. "It cost about R90 ($6) a month. I didn't even need a Virgin Active membership because I could gym at work for cheap," he recalls.

When Phake heard that RMB was going to replace the dated equipment at its gym, he asked the bank to donate it to a small fitness centre he wanted to open in Tembisa. His plan was to run it on the side and keep his banking job. "Although the equipment at RMB was old, it was still working fine. My idea was to refurbish it and clean it up," he says.

RMB agreed to donate the equipment if Phake would pay for the transport. But since he could not afford to move the heavy cardio and strength-training kit all the way to Tembisa, he decided to not take the venture further.

For the upgrade, RMB brought in an outside company to set up and manage the gym. Phake was amazed. "They came in with a new design and new equipment and literally ran it like a Virgin Active, except it was in our office building."

It got Phake's entrepreneurial juices flowing. He recognised that many other companies would probably also be interested in convenient on-site gyms for their employees. He tried to wrangle information from the owner of the company running the RMB gym. How did you do this? Who pays you? How much do you make from the gym? Would they be interested in partnering with him?

Even though the owner wasn't very forthcoming and was not interested in bringing the young banker on board, it didn't dampen Phake's enthusiasm. "I felt I could do it better than this guy. I began thinking of the possibilities. What if you had 50 to 100 of these gyms? It can actually be a real, proper business. And I wouldn't be competing with Virgin Active because they target a different market."

Around the same time, Phake met Kevin Payne, the CEO of PentaSystems, the South African distributor of Technogym, the Italian equipment found in most major health clubs. Phake told him of his interest in the industry and Payne took him under his wing. "He began showing me the ins and outs of the industry. I used to go to his offices and on Fridays he invited me along to networking events. I really started to learn what the industry is all about."

When Phake later revealed to Payne that he wanted to start his own gym-management company, he asked him to let him know if he heard of someone who wanted to open a gym. In exchange, Phake promised to purchase Technogym equipment.

Their agreement remains one of the reasons for Zenzele's success. Since PentaSystems has an inside track, Payne is well placed to introduce Phake to its clients who need someone to run their gyms while it helps them to sell more Technogym equipment.

DOING THE FIRST DEAL

With Zenzele little more than an idea, Phake raised R5 million (about $340 000) from the Awethu Project, a Johannesburg-based impact investment fund. While it is not common for investors to give money to such an early-stage business, Phake leveraged his financial background and won them over with his solid financial projections.

"Investors don't look for a great idea or one which gives people goose bumps, they look for an execution plan. If you're able to sit in the room and clearly show them a plan that will sustain the business for five, 10, 20 years, you are probably on your way to having a successful business," he explains.

Next came an opportunity in the form of South African Breweries (SAB), the country's largest beer maker. When the brewery contacted PentaSystems to buy equipment for a staff gym it was planning, Payne brought in Phake, who offered them a complete solution – from the equipment to the management of the gym. What made the deal even more attractive was that SAB could rent the equipment from Zenzele. This meant that the equipment, which depreciates over time, wouldn't sit on its books.

"We positioned ourselves as a full turnkey operator," Phake notes.

What also counted in Zenzele's favour is the fact that it is a 100 per cent black-owned entity and that companies are incentivised to procure from black-owned businesses in terms of South Africa's Broad-Based Black Economic Empowerment (BBBEE) codes.

SAB said yes and Phake was in business. The management fee he received from SAB indirectly subsidised the membership cost of the predominantly blue-collar workforce. "Those guys would not ordinarily be able to afford R600 ($41) per month for gym membership. And there we were, with a state-of-the-art facility that looks and feels like something you'd find anywhere in the world but at an affordable price," says Phake.

The gym saw a strong uptake and half the staff are still

using it. "That proves to me that people are very aspirational and conscious of their health, and that the reason they haven't used such facilities before is because they are too expensive," observes Phake.

Six months after launching Zenzele, Phake pulled off a major coup when he convinced Danny Gounden to join the company as its chief operating officer. Gounden had 15 years' experience at Virgin Active, including a stint as national operations manager. "Someone told me that Danny had just left Virgin Active and that they would introduce us. At the time, I didn't think much of it but once I met him I realised what he can do for Zenzele. He is a proper operator. He has opened a lot of health clubs and really understands what it takes. Danny definitely plays a big role. He makes me look good."

RIDING THE WELLNESS TREND

Following the success of the SAB gym, Phake was confident he had "a scalable business that could be replicated over and over again". Which is just what he did. In the next four years, Zenzele added Absa, Hollard Insurance, Rand Refinery and Alexander Forbes to its list of corporate clients. While the agreement with each client differs according to their budget, number of staff and existing infrastructure, the basic business model stays the same.

One of Zenzele's newest gyms is on the top floor of the insurance group Discovery's imposing head office in Johannesburg. The building has all the perks an employee could dream of: a supermarket, restaurants, dry cleaner, hair and beauty salon, basketball court, rooftop running track and, of course, a gym.

Discovery's founder and CEO Adrian Gore actively drives

employee wellness, explains Phake. "Companies like Discovery are forward-thinking. It is crazy to see the number of fitness events they hold at the office. They understand that people's productivity drops when they are unhealthy, which affects the bottom line. An active workforce is more productive and engaged, typically gets sick less often and is generally happier.

"We are not trying to build six-packs or prepare someone for a bodybuilding competition. It is about getting people to move since many don't exercise anymore. Your cardiorespiratory fitness is directly linked to your mortality. The more you move, the longer your life; the less you move, the shorter your life."

Like the SAB gym, the fees at the Discovery gym are low, too. Employees can use the facility for R200 ($14) per month. Phake points out that not all of the people who work at the building are high earners, and there are many employees – such as call centre agents – for whom the cost saving is significant.

Simply being in the Discovery building alone isn't enough to make the gym profitable, though. Zenzele's sales agents still have to pick up the phone and sell memberships. Each club functions as a separate business with a manager and agents who are incentivised to sell as many memberships to their gym as possible. The Discovery gym passed break-even point in its first year and stands at more than 3 000 members.

In addition to corporates, Zenzele also targets educational institutions and has a gym at the University of the Witwatersrand in Johannesburg, which currently has 5 000 members. Having a professional gym on campus, says Phake, makes the university more attractive to students.

Even so, he hasn't forgotten about his initial idea of running low-cost, independent gyms in underserved areas. Zenzele opened its first stand-alone gym in Musina on the Zimbabwe border. The second is set to launch soon in Acornhoek in Mpumalanga province. "It will be a 'dry gym' without pools and saunas but will be kitted out with modern equipment. It is also going to be tech-driven so that people can service themselves, which will reduce staff overheads," he explains.

Yet the company's biggest growth challenge is sourcing capital quickly enough to take advantage of opportunities as they present themselves. The equipment for a single gym alone can cost over $200 000. To ensure that one gym going through a rough patch doesn't impact the entire company's profitability, Zenzele treats each club as a separate entity and raises money specifically for that project.

A HIGH-GROWTH COMPANY IS A CONSCIOUS DECISION

Many entrepreneurs in Phake's shoes would have focused exclusively on the SAB gym for a year or so before looking to open a second facility. But Zenzele, which currently employs 80 people, has been able to grow relatively fast, especially considering that negotiations for a new gym can easily take 12 months to be concluded. Phake says the first time it hit him that he has an established company was when the bank approved a home loan against the salary he draws at Zenzele. "I was like, 'Okay, cool – I have a proper business'."

Phake believes that the reason for Zenzele's growth is the conscious decision he took right at the start to "build a big business with the potential to scale". He contrasts this with what he calls a "sole proprietor approach", such as a restaurateur who is happy to have one restaurant where they spend all their time and know most patrons by name.

He illustrates his point by telling of a would-be entrepreneur who pitched an idea for a spa business at an entrepreneurship event. "There are spas all over the place. What will make yours unique?" Phake asked her. "Because I give the best massages, like no one in the world," she replied.

He asked what would happen when she has five spas? Will she run from the one to the other to massage clients? She replied, "Oh, no, I will train my staff, but I still want to be the best."

"What I tried to say to her was that she, as the business owner, has to give the worst massages of everyone working there. You have to train your people to be the best because they have to do the job for you. As the owner, you have to think about growing the business and not massage people the whole day. If you do, it is all you will ever do and the company will never grow," he explains.

In his own business, Phake also had to resist the urge to become too involved in the day-to-day operations. "When I opened the SAB gym, someone actually told me that I would have to be the club manager. He said, 'Hey, Tumi, you'll have to open and close the gym and ensure there is paper in the toilet and that the floor isn't wet.'"

This is not the case. He quickly learnt that if he were to get involved in such minutiae, it would slow down the business growth. "My job is to find another SAB, and another one, and another one. Each year, I set myself the target to close a minimum of three to six projects. I bring in the business and then Danny takes it over and appoints teams to work at the gyms."

Now 80 per cent of his time is spent seeking new clients and finding investors. "I don't have to focus on operational issues. Danny and the team looks after that component. In fact, when I involve myself in things like that, Danny is quick to scold

me and say: 'You shouldn't be here. Get out and look for business.'"

4.

Monica Musonda

Instant noodle pioneer

By Jaco Maritz

In 2008, Zambian-born Monica Musonda moved to Nigeria to work for Aliko Dangote, founder of the Dangote Group and one of Africa's most successful businesspeople. With money borrowed from his uncle, Dangote started out by trading in products such as sugar, rice and pasta, and over the past 40 years built the company into a pan-African conglomerate with interests in cement, food, oil refining and property.

Musonda calls the experience of being a lawyer at the group similar to doing an MBA. In fact, she credits Dangote for inspiring her to take the leap to become an entrepreneur. As the group's director of legal and corporate affairs, she frequently accompanied him on business trips. "We visited Zambia a lot and every time we were there he would ask: 'Where are the Zambian businessmen? Why aren't there more, and why are they not taking up the opportunities?' He could clearly see the opportunities in Zambia and that's what encouraged me to see things differently here."

Dangote has often been described as a workaholic. In a 2012 speech at the Lagos Business School, he explained that he only needs about four to five hours' sleep. When travelling to China to attend a meeting or a conference for a few hours, he takes a commercial flight, he said, instead of his private plane, because the pilots need to rest for nine hours before their next flight. "I don't have nine hours. So, I take Emirates."

Musonda has first-hand experience of Dangote's hectic schedule. "He never stopped working, which meant we never stopped working. On the flip side, he emphasised the importance of maintaining humility and focus, being driven and working hard, and not being afraid to take calculated risks. His motto is 'nothing is impossible'."

FROM LAWYER TO ENTREPRENEUR

After obtaining a law degree at the University of Zambia, Musonda worked at the office of Zambia's Attorney General before leaving for the United Kingdom to obtain a master's degree at the University of London.

In 2000, she was back on the continent after accepting a job with Edward Nathan Sonnenbergs (now ENSafrica) in Johannesburg, South Africa. Starting as an associate, she moved through the ranks to become a director and led the firm's operations in Africa, advising clients such as mobile operator MTN, financial services firm Old Mutual and energy company Sasol on expansion projects.

But Musonda was seeking international experience, which is why, in 2006, she accepted a job with the International Finance Corporation in Washington DC. There she had the opportunity to work on projects as far afield as Asia and Latin America. However, she soon found the public sector nature of the job wasn't for her and, in 2008, left for Nigeria to join Dangote Group.

Living in Nigeria and working for Dangote forever changed

Musonda's perspective on entrepreneurship. "It opened my eyes to business, to the different opportunities that our continent offers and to a new way of thinking. What inspired me most about Nigeria was the entrepreneurial spirit, the fact that so many young people are taking the leap and working for themselves. They are not afraid to risk everything for what they believe in."

Six years later, Musonda took the plunge and returned to Lusaka to start Java Foods. It was – and still is, she says – not the done thing in Zambia to start your own business if you have a diploma or degree. Although many Zambians do have their own ventures, they are mostly necessity-driven entrepreneurs, such as informal traders, who lack other income or employment opportunities.

"For a very long time we were taught to work for somebody else. No one tells you that you can actually run your own business and that it's okay to do that. I think we don't believe that we can run a business and feel more comfortable working for someone else," Musonda explains. "Things are changing now but it's a slow process."

JUMPING INTO THE FOOD INDUSTRY

Despite having no experience in Zambia's food industry, which is dominated by multinationals, the first-time entrepreneur and her team pushed ahead and launched their first product, instant noodles called Eezee Noodles.

Many questioned whether Eezee Noodles, Zambia's first locally owned instant noodle brand, would be accepted and gain ground. After all, the multinationals dominating the sector in Zambia were introducing conventional foods and beverages, such as juices and snacks.

"People thought we were mad – that it wouldn't work," Musonda recalls.

Within three years, Eezee Noodles was Zambia's biggest instant noodle brand and it still accounts for 80 per cent of Java Foods' sales.

This does not mean there weren't missteps along the way. In the early days, Musonda wrongly assumed that everyone would be familiar with instant noodles and under-budgeted for marketing. "We assumed people would know what it was, and considering that it's cheap, that it would fly off the shelves. We were honestly surprised that people didn't know what we were selling. If we had done a little bit more homework, we would have known consumers need a little bit of education and would perhaps have saved ourselves a lot of money."

Her takeout from this is the importance of having a clear understanding of what consumers want, and how much they are willing to pay for it. Introducing completely new concepts can be risky business. "Ultimately, you could have great innovations, but if no one is willing to pay for something, it is not really a great idea."

A lack of reliable third-party market data in many African countries, which means companies have to learn about their industries as they go along, is partly to blame. Having been there, she now tells others, "You may not have all the answers, you may not know the size of the market, you may not know how much the competition is selling, but get in there and start gathering your own data. I would advise against spending a lot of money before you start to dig up lots and lots of information. Do some homework, but don't spend thousands and thousands of dollars on professional market research. You might not get the result you wanted and instead you would have wasted a lot of money and time."

To acquaint consumers with instant noodles, Java Foods started going to children's events to demonstrate how to prepare it and allow people to taste it.

After focusing exclusively on instant noodles for the first few years, in 2016, the company introduced fortified breakfast cereal made from maize and soya beans, followed by Num Nums, a maize snack, in May 2017.

"Java Foods is about providing affordable nutrition and using, as much as possible, local raw materials to make good, nutritious foods," Musonda says. Zambia has a high level of malnutrition and many people are either undernourished or overweight because, she believes, they don't know enough to distinguish between good and bad food.

TURBULENT BUSINESS ENVIRONMENT

When Java Foods was launched, the Zambian economy was roaring. Between 2008 and 2012, it expanded by an average of 8.1 per cent annually thanks to growth in industries such as agriculture, tourism, construction, manufacturing and mining (particularly copper).

However, around 2014, just as Musonda began finding her feet, the economy took a turn for the worse due to a plunge in copper prices, electricity shortages and falling agricultural output because of unfavourable weather. The power supply challenges had forced companies to invest in diesel generators, which meant the subsequent higher production costs were passed on to consumers and stoked inflation. To make matters worse, the value of the Zambian kwacha against the US dollar nosedived.

These economic headwinds – particularly the weak exchange rate and dramatic rise in interest rates – had a destabilising effect on Musonda's business. With interest rates on loans as high as 33 per cent, she was forced to seek alternative means of financing. "I spent much of 2017 looking for a strategic partner to take a significant stake in the company, so that we could worry less about the financing and focus more on growing the business."

Although Musonda believes that the worst of the economic slump is over, she doesn't expect a return to the rapid growth of the previous decade. "Now it is the survival of the fittest – those who are able to execute at affordable rates, who have scale, and who have access to technology and innovation."

She herself believes that to survive over the long term, bigger is better. "The reality is that to be a profitable, well-run business, it's all about scale. I've never had the ambition to be a small business and tell my staff they shouldn't think like an SME. If you think you will always be a small business, you will always be a small business."

Having said that, she advocates staying within your budget. "Ditch the fancy office and the fleet of the most expensive Toyotas. Start small, understand your revenue base and your expenses. When things stabilise, when you have a little bit of cash flow, then you can look into hiring that extra person, leasing a bigger warehouse, or buying more expensive equipment."

Java Foods currently imports its noodles and packages it at their plant in Lusaka, while the cereals and snacks are made at a local processing facility. Musonda's aim is to do all manufacturing in Zambia, but till then she has to contend with the significant challenges of importing product into a landlocked country. In the early days, she underestimated the transport costs and lead times. "Overland transportation in Zambia is really costly. You are held ransom by many transporters and they could absolutely kill your business. The reality turned out to be very different to what we had expected. In Africa, everything takes much longer than you think. Bringing in equipment, fixing stuff, getting electricity at your premises – it never happens as you'd planned."

As the Zambian food production industry grows, she hopes that others will recognise the opportunity in the packaging sector: "If we have a strong processing industry, the packaging industry should surely come up, too."

While many entrepreneurs dream of having a pan-African footprint, Musonda suggests first focusing on establishing the business locally. "Let people know your product in your home market – it has to have a home; it has to be from somewhere – before you start spreading yourself too thin by exporting."

So when is the optimal age to start a business? Musonda believes aspiring entrepreneurs should jump in sooner rather than later. "I would have loved to have been younger and have fewer commitments. At this stage, to fail would be a lot more painful than if I failed at 20 or 25 or 30, for instance. I think there is never a perfect scenario for you to start a business; but I think if you are going to take the leap, the earlier the better."

5.

Hassan Bashir

An insurance company created from nothing but grit and persistence

By Sven Hugo

The short story of Hassan Bashir's life goes like this: born to a pastoral farming family in rural Kenya, his parents' financial position did not allow him to attend secondary school. As a result, he began working in construction and doing other odd jobs immediately after finishing primary school. Eight years later, he used his savings to attend a preparatory school and write his secondary-school exams before registering at university, again partly paying his own way. After earning a degree in international business administration, he cofounded a successful insurance broking firm and then one of East Africa's largest information and communications technology (ICT) companies.

Now he is the founder and CEO of Takaful Africa Group, an Islamic insurance company, which, through its subsidiary Takaful Insurance of Africa (TIA), underwrites around $15 million annually.

"It's difficult to single out one particular thing that led me to where I am today," Bashir says. "I didn't follow the usual route."

TAKING RESPONSIBILITY FOR HIS OWN EDUCATION

Bashir began attending Leheley Primary School in Kenya's Wajir County at age eight and excelled academically. He started working his first job while at school, moving concrete building blocks on a construction site. "I was moving one block at a time and at the end of the month I received Ksh150, which today equates to $1.50. A third went to my father and a portion went towards my boarding fees for the next school semester," he recalls. "I also bought my first pair of shoes and a set of new clothes consisting of a shirt, pants and vest."

Despite finishing first in his class, his family could not afford to send him to secondary school. He continued working odd jobs ranging from waitering to construction. "I was essentially an expert builder, surveyor and manager when I was done," he says. But in the eight years, he never forgot his dream to finish school and attend university.

He read any book he could lay his hands on and, in 1990, after working for almost a decade, Bashir had saved up enough to register at the American High School, a preparatory school in Nairobi, and write the secondary-school final examination. His savings could pay for only three semesters at university though. "I enrolled at the United States International University – Africa (USIU – Africa) in Nairobi but had no idea what I would do once the three semesters were up," he says, "and by the end of 1994, I was out of money." He talked his way into a casual position as residents' assistant at USIU's housing office.

"Luckily, this turned into an acting position and then into a permanent appointment. The permanent job came with an officer's salary and two free courses under the university's Extended Tuition Waiver programme," he explains.

In 1996, Bashir graduated with a degree in international business administration, majoring in marketing. He talks appreciatively of USIU's "very open business-minded mentality" and its commitment to ingraining wealth creation and enterprise development into its students; something which further inspired him to start his own company as he had already begun preparing for it.

In the year he graduated, Kenyan politics was in complete disarray, which not only angered Kenyans but scared off foreign investors and created uncertainty for local businesses. "There were riots, students were protesting in the streets and the unemployment rate was very high, which caused foreign companies to exit the market," he says. Furthermore, neighbouring Somalia collapsed under an ongoing civil war that forced millions of Somalis to abandon their homes in search of security in other parts of the world. Kenya was their first stop.

"At the time, many younger people my age applied for economic refugee status in the United Kingdom or the United States," he says. "I was often asked what I was doing in Kenya and told to get out while I can." The decision to stay was not an easy one, Bashir says, but his plans never involved leaving Kenya.

Bashir's employers at the university were understandably bewildered when he announced his resignation from a safe full-time position on the day he graduated. He had a good degree but no job in a bad market – "a very bad market". He did have two plans, though. "One, to go into business. Two, I wanted to stay in Kenya. I had no other plans.

"By the end of the year I still hadn't done anything meaningful, but those months, though difficult, were my thinking months," explains Bashir. His thinking revolved around setting up a company with no seed capital and essentially devising a way to make a living from his energy, intellect and drive.

FIRST STEPS IN THE INSURANCE INDUSTRY

He cofounded Zawaam Insurance Brokers with Mohamed Abdi Affey, who later became a member of parliament and Kenya's ambassador to Somalia, and borrowed $300 to be able to pay the licensing fees. "In March 1997, we somehow had a company and we had our certificates. We were in business."

The Nairobi Yellow Pages, which listed most of the large companies in the country, provided them with the free ticket Bashir was looking for. "In those days, there were call boxes and each had a directory chained to it. I found a directory whose chain had been removed and took it to the office."

He designed a letterhead and drew on his marketing skills to create a brand. In the following months, Bashir wrote to 1 500 businesses listed in the directory. "I went from building to building and floor to floor to hand-deliver the letters," he says.

The first three months were painful. "We didn't insure one customer but I persisted until people came to know me," he says. "At the end of 1997, I had around 60 clients."

By 2002, Zawaam Insurance Brokers had 16 people in its employment and was a respected insurer. Bashir himself was the treasurer of the Association of Insurance Brokers of Kenya (AIBK).

SUCCESS REQUIRES A LONG-TERM VIEW

Bashir's MBA studies at USIU from 1998 to 2001 planted the seed for his next big venture. He took longer than others to complete his MBA as he had to divide his time between his studies and Zawaam. His thesis sought to understand the reasons a client would abandon one insurer for another and this exposed him to industry issues outside Kenya.

"Many of my Muslim clients also complained about insurance in general," he says. He took their complaints seriously and set out to find solutions. "Consumer behaviour is my bread and butter." While reading up, he came upon the Sharia-compliant Islamic insurance model, also known as takaful insurance. In an Islamic insurance scheme, members' contributions are pooled and invested, and claims are paid from this mutual fund, unlike a commercial insurance model where clients pay premiums directly to the insurer. In Islamic insurance, the funds remain the property of the members and the insurance company receives an administration fee only. At a specified time, the funds in the pool may be paid out as cash dividends or be put towards future contributions. This system provides an alternative to commercial insurance models, which are seen to violate Islamic restrictions on *riba* (interest), *maisir* (gambling) and *gharar* (uncertainty).

Despite talking to a top Kenyan scholar who convinced him to introduce Islamic insurance to the market, it was to be almost a decade before he finally did so.

"Success requires a long-term view. You have to build the foundation that will make you successful five or 10 years from now. It's easy to only see the money early on and make mistakes. I see many start-ups that cut corners when they are in a hurry to meet their obligations. They conform to mediocrity and fail on service delivery, all to save a buck."

Instead, Bashir sold his stake in Zawaam Insurance Brokers in 2002 and cofounded Soliton Telmec with business partner Abdirahman Sheikh. Today, the ICT company is East Africa's

largest network integrator and builder and provider of telecommunications infrastructure, with offices in Uganda, Djibouti
and Kenya. It has around 300 employees and an annual
turnover of between $10 and $15 million.

While seeing to the survival of Soliton, the idea of Islamic
insurance continued milling around in his thoughts. In 2004,
two years after founding Soliton, Bashir presented the first concept paper on his Islamic insurance plan to the CIC Insurance
Group in Nairobi. "I wanted to introduce the product through
an existing company," he explains, which is why he entered
into talks with CIC's CEO at the time, Nelson Kuria. Kuria was
enthusiastic about the idea but his board was uncomfortable
with the risk- and profit-sharing model and declined. "It was
disappointing," says Bashir. "It threw me. I thought my idea
would never come to fruition." It was Kuria who persuaded
him to work towards a fully-compliant, stand-alone Islamic
insurance company – "it was a total mind shift".

"He was right," says Bashir: a fully fledged Islamic insurance company was the next step. "I met with my business partner at Soliton and asked for his support. I was very surprised
when he said, 'Go ahead. What do you need?'" He needed an
actuary, an accountant, an underwriter and a lawyer. So Bashir
put together a team and they worked out of Soliton's "back-
yard".

Bashir's business partnerships are based on ethics, integrity
and transparency. "Businesses succeed when you choose the
right friends and partners, and when you base your entire business philosophy on these values," he says. But that's not all.
"It's critical that you deliver a product or service that the market needs," he stresses. Entrepreneurs have to pick apart their
business idea and know the sector they wish to target intimately

– and "then you have to pitch for it and stay with it. It's not enough to be a nice guy if you have nothing to offer. You must offer people a product that will appeal to them and will fill a need."

While the business plan for Takaful Insurance of Africa (TIA) bounced around at the Kenyan insurance regulators, Bashir went about raising capital for the company. They also began to train their staff. "We were financing diploma-level training in Kuala Lumpur, Sri Lanka, Bahrain and Kenya for at least 15 people. In addition to persuading the regulators and raising funds, we furthered knowledge of the Islamic insurance market by training people."

In 2011, TIA was granted a licence as a general underwriter.

"We have proven to the insurance industry and the general public that it is possible for an insurance company to share its profits with policyholders under the takaful model and remain viable as a business," Bashir wrote in the company's 2012 annual report. TIA today employs 230 people in Kenya and Somalia. Although it is Sharia-compliant, TIA is open to everyone.

In 2016, TIA partnered with the International Livestock Research Institute (ILRI) to provide insurance to farming communities in the arid and semi-arid northern and eastern parts of Kenya, Bashir's birthplace. There are also plans to expand into Djibouti, Tanzania and Uganda, where low insurance penetration numbers indicate a big opportunity for them.

When the low times came around, and there were many, when he couldn't pay rent or properly feed himself, not continuing never occurred to Bashir. "The most important thing a young entrepreneur needs is staying power," he says. "Don't be 'temporary' minded." There's a reason why businesses don't simply hand start-ups a cheque, he notes, and it's something start-ups tend to overlook. "Clients want delivery, and if the ink on your corporation certificate is still wet, no one knows whether you are still going to be around the next day. You have to show them you are here to stay. It's very easy to drop out, but don't panic, success isn't something that shows up immediately. Don't run away."

It took him a decade to make good on the promise he had made himself to create his Islamic insurance company, and sometimes he wishes it hadn't taken so long. Perhaps if there had been incubators, advisors and more general advice in those years … "but success depends on integrity and delivery".

"I went to market a young, energetic, extremely dedicated businessperson, but I was also a very honest businessperson. I kept every promise I had made, whether it be a service promise or payment promise. You want clients to say, 'If it's Hassan, we believe him.' This has to happen again and again and again and again. You want it to happen throughout your life. Success is a lifelong aspiration, it's not something you do once."

6.

Ebele Enunwa

A $50-million food and retail empire

By Dianna Games

Ebele Enunwa's two companies – Sundry Foods and Sundry Markets – own 30 restaurants dotted around Nigeria, a corporate catering business, two factory bakeries as well as a grocery retail chain comprising six modern supermarkets with another six under construction. He employs more than 1 700 people and expects to generate close to $50 million in revenue in 2018.

However, becoming an entrepreneur wasn't his original plan. Enunwa's early vision of life after school was influenced by the fact that his parents were both professionals; his mother worked in primary healthcare and his father was a partner at the international accounting firm PricewaterhouseCoopers (PwC). The young Ebele wanted to be a professional too, and specifically an accountant, emulating his father whom he idolised.

PwC was one of five international accounting firms in Nigeria but he didn't want to work at the same firm as his father. "The only other one I had an interest in working with was Arthur Andersen, then a prestigious global accounting firm. After I failed to get a place there, I thought my world had fallen apart. I had no plan B."

When Arthur Andersen closed its doors after a corporate

scandal in the United States a few years later, Enunwa realised that accounting job was never part of his future, and that "every disappointment is an opportunity in disguise".

Although he had no particular interest in the financial sector, his attention was drawn to Investment Banking & Trust Company (IBTC), an investment bank formed in 1989, which his accountant friends talked about enthusiastically. He applied for a job there and was accepted. Enunwa joined the relatively small team of about 40 in their office in Lagos headed by the bank's founder, Atedo Peterside, a household name in the Nigerian corporate world. IBTC was later bought by South African banking giant Standard Bank and became Stanbic IBTC Bank.

"I never wanted to be a banker but it sounded like an interesting opportunity," he says. Enunwa quickly worked his way up through the ranks. After just two years at the head office in Lagos, he was transferred to Port Harcourt, the fast-growing centre of Nigeria's oil and gas industry, to head up one of IBTC's two new regional offices.

The move turned out to be life-changing. "We were a three-person team and I had to learn about the bank's wider business." He dealt with big transactions, met and worked with political and business leaders, managed pension and private wealth funds and was part of the privatisation of state assets. It made him feel as if he was helping to shape a modernising, growing Nigeria. "It was a big responsibility for someone in his twenties," he says.

Born and bred in Lagos, Enunwa had never been to Port Harcourt, an hour's flight from his home town, before. Once in the bustling southern city, he noticed that Port Harcourt, unlike Lagos and some other cities in Nigeria, had few hospitality and leisure outlets. The hotels were of a poor standard and people mostly had their meals at home. Oil was the only game in town.

"I had travelled a bit in the course of my career and had been a customer in hotels and restaurants. I grew up in a city with all these amenities. I am a 'work hard, play hard' kind of guy. I wanted to live in an environment where there were options to relax and unwind after work. Port Harcourt didn't have many places of the type and quality I was accustomed to.

"When faced with such challenges, I believe you have two options: you either sulk and run away or do something about it. I chose the latter and decided to see if I could build a business to contribute to the city's hospitality industry. I initially thought about setting up a business on the side and getting a manager. My plan was to keep my banking job and oversee my own projects after hours."

It soon became apparent that this would not work and he had to make a commitment. "Besides," he says, "I grew up in an environment where I learnt that if something had to be done, it had to be done properly."

He started big and approached Hilton Hotels, the international chain, to see if they would be interested in a management contract for a hotel in Port Harcourt, a bold move for an aspirant hotelier. It turned out that the group was interested in growing its footprint in Nigeria, but to get such a hotel up and running, Enunwa needed $15 million in start-up capital – a major roadblock for a young man embarking on his first venture.

As a result, he moved into the fast food industry, thinking it would be easier and cheaper to get started. He raised the initial capital from family and friends, the first investors in his new business. "Family and friends know what you are capable of and they know what they are putting their money into. It is not easy to convince a stranger or someone who doesn't know you to give you money," he says. "Providence begins at home."

He calls it "a case of luck meeting opportunity". One of his friends put a property he had leased for a similar venture into Enunwa's new business as equity. At the same time, the Central Bank of Nigeria directed banks in the country to set aside 10 per cent of their profits to fund small and medium-sized enterprises. Enunwa was in pole position and Standard Trust Bank took a 40 per cent stake in his proposed venture – a national chain of food outlets headquartered in Port Harcourt.

Although his business plan called for start-up capital of $2 million, Enunwa was able to raise only about $1 million but nonetheless decided to proceed.

FAST FOOD JOURNEY

The original idea was to buy into a foreign franchise. As a qualified accountant with banking experience, Enunwa felt the franchise route held the most promise. "We tried McDonald's but it wasn't interested in Nigeria at the time. KFC didn't even respond to our enquiry and South African franchise Nando's was already in talks with a possible Nigerian partner."

Eventually he was led to the Nigerian franchise holder of an international fast food brand that had outlets in Lagos. It seemed like an ideal partnership but then he found out that the company was involved in a dispute with the international brand owner. It got worse. While Enunwa was luring investors with the promise of an international franchising brand, the franchisor pulled out of Nigeria because of the dispute.

Their local partner quickly set up another fast food brand and passed it off to Enunwa. "The company was a mess. They were not prepared and had not perfected their recipes or their supply chain," he says. "He also expected the same fees and royalties for the new brand as for the international franchise. It no longer made commercial sense.

"It was a disaster for us as we had secured investors who had already begun to invest with us. We couldn't return the money and my credibility was at stake. It was a tough challenge to face so early in the business.

"The other company was well known in Nigeria and as a result I had let my guard down, believing I was on solid ground. It was not an amicable separation and I was quite shaken by the experience."

He may have been shaken but Enunwa wasn't deterred and decided he had to move forward by launching his own brand. That brand was Kilimanjaro, a chain of fast food restaurants serving local meals to international standards.

Why the name? "We wanted a quintessential African name that also pointed to where we wanted to go: to the top of Africa.

"As we only had half the start-up capital, we couldn't pursue the planned rollout. In 2004, we started with one restaurant in Port Harcourt and struggled to grow the restaurant count due to lack of capital."

They have since rolled out dozens of restaurants across the country, including Lagos, where there is stiff competition from local and international chains such as KFC and Domino's Pizza.

Rice and chicken are the biggest sellers in Nigeria but Enunwa also added local dishes such as beans, plantain, yam and catfish. The Kilimanjaro chain offers dine-in and takeaway services and recently launched an e-commerce delivery service. He expects this will anchor the company's growth. "Deliveries currently account for less than five per cent of restaurants' revenue but this is expected to grow. We need to perfect the logistics in terms of timing, payment systems and ensure the service is fully reliable."

There are no plans to franchise the Kilimanjaro brand at the moment. He says, "I had a bad experience with franchising and wouldn't want to put anyone else through it. When we do decide to franchise, we will do it right. We will be sure to have a strong value proposition for a franchisee."

He also built up a corporate catering venture with 12 contract catering locations and two factory bakeries on the back of the restaurant business. Both operate as divisions of the company and service thousands of customers daily, contributing approximately 20 per cent of the company's revenue.

TAKING ON THE RETAIL GIANTS

In 2013, Enunwa saw an opportunity in grocery retailing and decided to venture into this area with a string of supermarkets borrowing the Sundry branding and established a new company – Sundry Markets. The supermarkets trade as Marketsquare.

It was while researching business opportunities for his wife, Nancy – also a former banker with Stanbic IBTC Bank – that Enunwa woke up to the opportunities in modern grocery retailing. In Nigeria, this has been driven by South African retailers Shoprite and Game which, together with the Spar franchise, had fewer than 20 stores and accounted for about three per cent of the retail industry at the time. "Nigerians had begun to embrace modern retail but the forerunners were barely scratching the surface. One of the players suggested the market could absorb over 500 modern retail stores. The goal was wide open."

Additional research indicated that a domestic company

would be better poised to succeed and outperform a foreign retailer, given their local knowledge. The research showed that while traditional retail outlets (such as markets,
kiosks, table-top sellers and street hawkers) were still dominating the field and accounted for over 95 per cent of sales, modern supermarkets would continue to grow while traditional outlets slowed down.

"I had also observed several synergies between our Sundry Foods businesses and that of modern grocery retailing. Prepared foods and bakery operations were embedded in modern retailers' store formats and appeared to account for up to 15 per cent of their revenue. In actual fact, we were already in direct competition with them, particularly in malls where both of us were present."

This time it was easier to raise capital on the back of Sundry Foods' success. Enunwa engaged a British retail consulting firm to plan the stores. He then approached the investors in Sundry Foods to back his new venture. Leveraging his entire investment in Sundry Foods, he was able to raise about $10 million in equity from his investors and a private equity firm.

"I was not going to make the same mistake twice. Unlike Sundry Foods, where we started with half the capital and battled to raise additional money for many years, I was determined to raise all the capital to fulfil my business plan before start-up."

The first Marketsquare supermarket opened in 2015 in Bayelsa State, not far from Port Harcourt, in the state capital, Yenagoa. Enunwa specifically chose the city because of its small size – around 280 000 inhabitants – and because there were no modern retailers. Plus, he had access to land there.

He used this store to iron out teething problems and perfect the model. "Grocery retailing is fundamentally more difficult than the food service business. It is bigger and there are lots of moving parts," he says.

"We made a lot of errors but were able to sort them all out. For instance, air-conditioning and refrigeration in our first store took six months to install and still didn't function properly when we opened. Port Harcourt would have been much less forgiving."

SURVIVING NIGERIA

Nigeria is known for being one of Africa's toughest business environments. Its poor power supply and erratic connections to the national power grid mean that companies often have to install their own generators. Sundry Foods' average monthly electricity bill is about five per cent of revenue, excluding the cost of maintenance on generators. The businesses run on generators around 10 hours a day. Similarly, companies have to supplement or find alternatives to other services such as water supply.

Local suppliers with sufficient capacity and stock to provide raw materials or inputs are difficult to find. "Many are quite opportunistic and have not invested in the necessary infrastructure to handle the increasing demands from growing businesses. They lack capital but, more importantly, they lack knowledge. Sourcing from small-scale farmers is challenging as they are difficult to find and many are out of touch with modern business dealings," says Enunwa.

Fresh meat is one of Sundry Foods' key inputs but high-quality livestock is in short supply. Enunwa explains it is difficult to find quality, reliable suppliers among local farmers, given their poor feedstock, veterinary back-up and funding, and a lack of proper abattoir facilities and cold storage. This is exacerbated by infrastructure deficits and Nigeria's infamous traffic congestion which can play havoc with the supply chain and logistics.

Consequently, the company sources meat from vendors and leaves the headache of finding stock to them. It may not always be of the quality people elsewhere are used to, but it is what Nigerians know and eat at home.

On top of that, Enunwa – and other Nigerian business owners – has to deal with the overzealous application of regulations. "The authorities seem to be more concerned about generating revenue for themselves than food safety, and harassment levels are at times high. We are currently considering setting up a unit just to deal with that."

Till now, Nigeria's food and retail industries have lagged those of developed countries and as a result, Sundry Foods decided to train staff from scratch to compensate for the skills shortage. Its well-trained staff now counts as one of the company's competitive advantages.

Many Nigeria-based companies were badly affected by the recession of 2016 and 2017, which spawned a serious foreign exchange crisis. Enunwa's strategy to source from local vendors helped to tide him over during this time.

The Nigerian economy was further buffeted by a 300 per cent devaluation in the Nigerian naira, which lasted several months. This led to consumer price spikes and many shoppers pulled back on non-essential spending such as phone upgrades and television sets.

He says the Nigerian market is highly price sensitive and retailers have to be careful about their pricing, as even a small shift can quickly lead to a loss of market share. That is why he believes in building a diverse portfolio of products and services.

NO EXPERIENCE IS WASTED

Although he had never wanted to be a banker, Enunwa says the experience he gained at IBTC has been invaluable. "If you don't understand finance, how can you run a business?" he asks.

Raising capital is difficult for new entrepreneurs but it is critical to get what you need in the beginning, even if it takes time. The fact that Sundry Foods launched with half the planned capital has compromised its business plan and projections. "The first four or five years' growth was stymied by our limited budget. Growth was small, slow and bitter."

Most banks were still unwilling to lend money to food service businesses because they did not take them seriously and saw restaurants and catering companies as entertainment rather than the retail end of the agriculture value chain. It was a young industry and the few players didn't have a long track record.

Sundry Foods' first real break came when United Kingdom-based private equity firm Silk Invest came on board in 2012. "After eight years of being undercapitalised and hobbling along, we could finally run." Later, a second private equity firm, Sango Capital, invested in Sundry Markets.

"To reach critical mass, you need money but those who can give you money to reach that critical mass want to see the viability of the business first and so you end up chasing your tail unless you have a proven asset already," says Enunwa, explaining the catch 22 situation many entrepreneurs find themselves in.

Because Sundry Markets was properly capitalised, it grew

much more quickly than Sundry Foods. "Even though it is only in its third year, Sundry Markets is quickly catching up to the revenues of the other business, which has been trading since 2004."

So, has he achieved his aim of providing leisure options for Nigerians? "I think so. We have become an indispensable part of people's lives. They now have options to eat out and busy people can enjoy good food without spending hours preparing it.

"We are definitely the market leader in Port Harcourt and growing in Lagos and Abuja, the capital. We operate in 10 other cities and have a high concentration in the country's southern region. Data indicates that Sundry Foods is in the top five food services players in Nigeria, and we are building Sundry Markets up to become one of the four largest grocery retailers in the country by 2020."

Enunwa hopes to build a billion-dollar business out of Africa. "The way I see it, we have already grown our business 50 million times considering that we started from zero. Getting to $1 billion means we just need to grow it by another 20 times."

As for his dream of building a world-class hotel, he hasn't let it go entirely. "I don't know if it will ever happen as there is so much to chew on at the moment; but rest assured that if I do venture into that area, I intend to make a spectacular landing in the industry which sparked my interest in entrepreneurship so many years ago."

7.

Tayo Oviosu

The entrepreneur who traded in his Silicon Valley life to bring mobile money to unbanked Nigerians

By Jeanette Clark

In an alternate universe, one of Nigeria's most successful mobile financial services providers, Paga, does not exist. Instead, Tayo Oviosu looked at the list of entrepreneurial ideas he drafted six months after arriving back in the country from studying and working in the United States, and chose item number one: start a members-only club in Lagos.

There is a smile in his voice when he recalls this list and the fact that the first entry of about 20 options was so completely different from the path he ultimately chose.

"Three months after writing the list, I decided to focus on what has today become Paga. It was number 10 – *mobile payments*; number 11 was *banking the unbanked*. And there is actually a note that these two go together with a line connecting them to number three, which was *a cloud payroll solution*. Today we offer all three," the 40-year-old founder and CEO of Paga recalls.

The private members' club did not fall by the wayside entirely either. Oviosu is one of the governors of the Capital Club Lagos and is actively involved on the social side. "Like all ideas on the list, it was valid, but clearly the one for Paga percolated in my mind," he says.

Just over 10 years ago, the Nigerian-born Stanford University graduate was working in San Francisco, California, on a team at Cisco Systems for corporate development (providing venture capital) in four technology sectors: virtual computing, application networking, security and network management. His career was flourishing; he was working on multimillion-dollar investments and acquisitions. He was living the life in Silicon Valley. Then he moved back to Nigeria.

"I had a very successful career, yes," he says, "but I always had strong intentions to come back to Nigeria."

Oviosu grew up at a time when Nigeria was beginning to achieve its potential as the giant of Africa. He also saw the country starting to lose that shine.

"I always wanted to be part of the country's redevelopment but along the way in the United States, I lost that drive a little. I was comfortable with my life and career as a venture capitalist." His friends, however, kept encouraging him to come back. In 2007, one of them said that the Nigeria of the day felt like India and China 15 years prior: untapped potential everywhere.

"That really inspired me. Most of the companies that had existed in India in the nineties were now highly successful conglomerates." He decided to come back and, in 2008, joined a private equity firm in Lagos. However, it wasn't long before he felt the urge to pave his own way and become part of the narrative of a newly booming Nigeria.

GETTING RID OF THE CASH

Today, Paga has over nine million users. Compared with the

largest bank in Nigeria which has 12 million customers, the growth it has experienced in less than a decade is phenomenal.

"I am very proud of what we have achieved. In the beginning we had an ambitious goal – fifteen by fifteen, we called it. It was way too ambitious and we clearly didn't achieve it. Yet, even though we hadn't signed up 15 million users by 2015, we have reached a significant number of people," he says.

Oviosu believes Paga's success cannot be counted in the number of users only. For example, the volume of transactions also augments this upwards trajectory. The company processed 94 000 transactions during August 2012 and 2.6 million during May 2018. That amounts to an increase of 2 665 per cent over six years.

Not that it was plain sailing all the time. The business officially started in April 2009 and they had a working product in September 2010 but had to wait until November 2011 to get a full licence to operate. "After getting the licence, we could raise money from venture firms and finally, in August 2012, Paga launched properly," Oviosu explains.

He was lucky enough to have funding throughout the first three and a half years, thanks to angel investors and Alitheia Capital/Goodwell, a fintech venture capital firm. It allowed them to weather the period when income was scarce but payments and expansion investment had to be made. "I recently said to my team that, knock on wood, it has been almost 10 years – and we have always been able to pay all salaries every month."

Profitability, however, arrived only five years after Paga's launch, in the second quarter of 2017 and came about after Oviosu had an *aha* moment in 2014. He realised that, contrary to the business models found in Silicon Valley, profitability has to come before growth when operating in a country such as Nigeria.

"Until then I was largely focused on growth. When I decided to change direction, I also knew I did not want to achieve this by slashing the workforce. So, we set ourselves the goal of becoming profitable before the end of 2017. We managed to show a profit earlier than that and have sustained it since then," he says.

ALLOWING CIRCUMSTANCES TO DRIVE AND NOT DETER YOU

In the summer of 1993, the year Oviosu finished secondary school, the result of the first Nigerian presidential elections since the military coup 10 years prior was annulled by head of state General Ibrahim Badamasi Babangida. This led to riots and all universities in the country were shut down. With no university to go to, Oviosu began looking for a solution that would benefit his plans, instead of seeing the situation as an insurmountable obstacle.

In 1994, he left to study abroad, being accepted into a junior college in California. There, he worked five jobs to support himself. He did not let financial difficulties deter him and obtained an electrical engineering degree from the University of Southern California and his master's in business administration from Stanford University.

His childhood, and especially his entrepreneur single mom, formed him as a person and as a businessman. "Seeing her raise five kids by herself and sacrifice so many things for us, has definitely made me ask, 'Why not?' It taught me that I could also go into business."

The decision on mobile money and payments as his calling

was inspired by circumstance, and the frustration caused by those circumstances. At the time of his return, and to a large extent still today, Nigeria was a cash-driven society. This continues to be the reality for the estimated 60 million unbanked and underbanked Nigerians who are excluded from the digital financial ecosystem. Almost half of the entire population of 196 million is further excluded from basic financial services. A year after Paga was properly launched to market, a report published in the *Afro Asian Journal of Social Sciences* estimated that 99 per cent of customer transactions in Nigerian banks were cash, be it over the counter or at an automated teller machine (ATM).

Having to carry around wads of cash to transact frustrated Oviosu along with his fellow countrymen. "For people to get out of poverty and for Nigeria to become the giant it could be, Nigerians need access to financial services," he says. As an example, to send money to relatives in a faraway town more often than not meant entrusting the cash to a bus driver.

Paga started mainly as a money transfer service before adding bills and accounts payments. This year, Paga will double down on its person-to-person transfers and savings offerings. Then comes opening Paga's agent network to the banks as well as launching loans.

All this is done through a countrywide network of over 17 000 agents. Paga's goal is to have 80 000 by 2020. These small businesses or entrepreneurs form the core of Paga's business, often seeing an increase of foot traffic to their stores when they partner with the mobile money company. They are Paga's competitive advantage and its secret sauce, acting like human ATMs along with offering the other services such as sending and receiving money, paying bills and buying airtime. In a country where cash is king, having a familiar face as the Paga agent in your community (someone you have purchased goods from for a number of years) helps to build trust and convince people to switch to a mobile money environment. Agents receive commission on every Paga transaction they perform for their customers.

For those who are banked, Paga acts as a complement to their accounts. Because a user can link their bank accounts and cards to a Paga wallet, it eliminates the need to give out this sensitive information and greatly lowers the risk of theft or fraud. It also does away with having to first deposit money into a Paga wallet to make payments. Instead, a specified account or card is debited, making Paga function much like Paypal or Venmo. It works in Nigeria because the bulk of the ATMs in the country are in cities but Paga allows users to transact from their accounts from anywhere in the country.

STAYING FOCUSED AND STRETCHING YOUR GOALS

In its infancy, Paga had to bide its time and rein in the dream to offer a full suite of financial services to the unbanked to first ensure that consumers are ready for these products.

"We learnt to follow the market. Our chief technology officer often speaks about 'appropriate technology'. When he says that, he is referring to a tech offering that matches the current need of the customer," Oviosu says.

Nigerians also don't appreciate companies or products that chop and change. "The market does not reward too much flip-flopping and not being focused. You have to be dogged and extremely focused on what you are doing. You also have to think about sustainability, even if it comes at the expense of growth. In Silicon Valley one can throw money at research and development and growth; here, you have to become profitable quickly."

When asked whether it's better to set ambitious or realistic objectives for a business, Oviosu turns to running, another of his passions, and Eliud Kipchoge's attempt to become the first athlete to run a marathon in under two hours. The Kenyan marathon champion and two other African athletes attempted to do this at the Monza Formula 1 track in Milan on 6 May 2017. After three years' planning and training, Kipchoge finished in 2 hours 25 seconds.

"I watched him miss his goal by 25 seconds. Having a too-ambitious goal would be like me saying I want to hit the two-hour marathon mark. I ran my first marathon last year in six hours! I have to be realistic. It is a fine balance as you want to stretch yourself as well as push the team. Fundamentally, I believe that if you have high expectations for yourself and your team, they will step up to meet them."

It stands to reason, then, that his favourite African proverb, which he uses often, goes: "If you want to go fast, go alone. If you want to go far, go together."

"One of the things I am adamant about is sharing and being transparent with the team about what we are trying to achieve and why. We have a joint mission that goes beyond simply making money. It is to become one of the largest companies in the country, solve payments and financial inclusion, and having a significant impact on this continent. The next step is to take Paga outside of Africa to ultimately make it simple for one billion people to access and use money, that's the goal," he says.

This impact, first and foremost, consists of making it easy for people to pay and get paid. "Five years from now I want to be able to tell a supermarket cashier, 'Just Paga it'; or to hear on the streets, 'Just Paga me'." #JustPagaIt is one of the hashtags peppering Paga's Twitter feed to familiarise followers with the concept.

Secondly, Oviosu wants to "create an army of entrepreneurs" by growing Paga's network of agents, all of whom receive commission on the transactions they handle; thus earning an income or supplementing their existing shop's revenue while attracting new customers to it by virtue of being a Paga agent.

"So far we have created 240 direct jobs and approximately 10 000 indirect jobs. Some of our top agents have 12 employees. That is the legacy we are hoping to leave behind."

In the second half of 2018, Paga raised an additional $10 million to explore expansion to countries like Ethiopia, Mexico and the Philippines.

THE IMPATIENT, FURIOUSLY FLAPPING DUCK

Asked about his own competitive advantage as an entrepreneur, Oviosu is silent as he first has to think about it. He talks passionately about his business, his team, his country – but talking about himself does not come quite as easy.

"I just try to do my best as a person. I am passionate about what I do. I try and do right by everyone. I am like a duck on water – very calm on the outside, but under the surface I am flapping my feet very, very hard as I constantly think about things, trying to rise above different problems."

Does that mean he struggles to switch off? "Yes," he admits. "Trying to shut down is hard for me." So much so, that one of the unique techniques he uses to relax, other than running, is mentoring.

"There are a handful of companies where I help the leadership teams with their businesses. I see a lot of value in mentoring and am actively involved. In this way, I still use my intellectual capacity but my mind gets to focus on something other than Paga." For a moment, the duck gets to flap in a different pond.

Discipline, openness and transparency: these are three attributes Oviosu lists with regard to his own leadership style. He describes his approach to leading a team as more than extractive. "It is my responsibility to keep the lights on; to provide a place for them to grow."

He is not shy to admit that the flapping duck is not very patient. "Things take unnecessarily long in Nigeria. Why do people want to meet in person all the time? I often suggest a call, or video-conferencing, but it is not the done thing yet." Patience is, however, important for doing business in the environment Paga operates in.

"My co-founder, Jay Alabraba, is much more patient. There are some situations where I know he should be the one driving," he admits, "and then I let him take charge."

NIGERIA: A LONG-TERM VIEW REQUIRED

Oviosu's brand of ambitious optimism combined with taking a realistic view comes to the fore when discussing Nigeria and its future. What's missing, he believes, is a plan. Something like South Korea's 100-year plan which the government of the day adheres to, regardless of politics.

There are signs of it in Nigeria, but things are changing slower than initially anticipated. Oviosu nevertheless cautions against being cynical. "If you step back and look at the bigger picture, you will see advances. For the first time there are social programmes in place. The government has developed, and, more importantly, publicised a strategy to diversify away from oil.

"I believe that Nigeria can regain its shine but it will be much tougher than I thought. I don't think Nigeria will become the giant it could be in my lifetime. I am realistic enough to know it is a multi-generational effort. My generation simply has the opportunity to lay the foundation and I, and Paga, would have been part of that."

8.

Navalayo Osembo

How to make a Kenyan running shoe

By Iga Motylska

Why does a country renowned for its Olympic medallist runners not have its own professional running shoe?

For 33-year-old Navalayo Osembo and her business partner, Weldon Kennedy, this question led them to found Enda Athletic, a Kenyan running shoe and sportswear company.

Hailing from a village two hours outside Eldoret in the west of Kenya, Osembo grew up in, as she calls it, "running country". Eliud Kipchoge, the reigning Olympic marathon champion and winner of eight consecutive marathons, lives there with his wife and children. Eldoret and nearby towns such as Kaptagat and Iten are where professional athletes from across the globe, such as Britain's Olympic gold-medallist Mohamed 'Mo' Farah and three-time London Marathon winner Paula Radcliffe, have travelled to train at high altitude. It is also where local athletes such as David Rudisha and Mary Keitany prepare for races. This high-lying area along the edge of the Rift Valley has several long-distance running trails and is dotted with training camps. Training at high altitudes, where the air is rarefied, produces more red blood cells to aid oxygen delivery to the muscles, allowing athletes to perform better at lower altitudes.

Osembo met Kennedy, an American communications and campaign strategist living in Kenya, in 2015 at a business accelerator, where she pitched an idea she had for a sports academy in western Kenya.

She calls it a "meeting of the minds". They spoke of manufacturing a running shoe that celebrates Kenya's legacy as the home of Olympic long-distance runners. "At our first formal meeting, a week later, we spoke about it for so long that we knew we were going to do it," recalls Osembo.

They also had a name for their company – Enda, the Kiswahili word for *go* and the cheer with which Kenyans spur on their athletes.

But neither knew the first thing about designing or manufacturing running shoes.

For the next six months, Osembo and Kennedy dedicated themselves to intensive research: collecting data, studying industry reports, watching YouTube tutorials on designing and assembling running shoes, and holding regular brainstorming sessions.

They interviewed prominent Kenyan athletes to learn about the technical and aesthetic aspects they consider when buying running shoes and how existing shoes could be improved. "We reached out to a lot of people in the industry, including shoe designers and manufacturers, who shared valuable information and referred us to others who could help," says Osembo.

The Iten, Enda's first shoe, is a lightweight design ideally suited for runs of up to 20km and honours Kenya's running tradition through its name and design. The town of Iten was also where Osembo and Kennedy put their prototype shoes to the test. Here they received the most valuable constructive feedback from athletes, such as Joan Cherop Massah and Justin Lagat, who tested the shoes and provided technical feedback that led to numerous iterations before the final product.

The shoe has a 4mm drop, which means it has 4mm more cushioning in the heel than in the front of the foot, to allow runners to emulate the Kenyan barefoot running style and ensure natural landing strides. The midsole cups the heel to ensure that the shoe wraps snugly around the foot and the wider toe box allows a runner's toes to splay. "We wanted it to feel as if you are barefoot and that the shoes give the feeling of flying," Osembo says.

Osembo and Kennedy incorporated several Kenyan historical references and cultural elements into the design. The Iten shoes are currently available only in the three colours of the Kenyan flag. A spear, the symbol of the country's freedom on the national coat of arms, is emblazoned on the side and points forward, "urging runners to go, run, find, discover, explore and be". The rift cut into the back of the heel is a nod to the Rift Valley and its legacy as the home of champions, says Osembo. Twelve lines cut into the side of the midsole represent 12 December, Jamhuri Day, on which Kenya celebrates its independence from the United Kingdom in 1963. Kenya's motto – *Harambee*, Kiswahili for *we all pull together* – is etched into the bottom of the sole.

CROWDFUNDING CAMPAIGN

By the time the Iten was ready for production, Enda had no money left. They struggled to get funding the traditional way as banks wanted six months' payslips or business assets as surety. Alternative funding streams also proved difficult because Enda was in the early stages of operation. Investors first wanted to see more cash inflow, which they didn't have.

Osembo wouldn't let that stop them. Instead, they made a video and turned to the internet to crowdfund the business. Their Kickstarter and Indiegogo campaigns ran from May 2016 to July 2017 and raised $140 000 from over 1 000 backers in 32 countries across five continents – almost double the requested amount of $75 000. It allowed them to produce the first 2 000 pairs of shoes and start the second production run for another 6 000 pairs.

The experience taught them valuable lessons. First, Osembo says, a crowdfunding campaign page has to be detailed and contain as much information as possible. It should give backers a sense of involvement in the product's creation and production process through regular updates. Enda maximised traffic to its page with quality editorial and video content, email newsletters, organic and paid social media and by advertising and securing press coverage, specifically in sports media. While most backers contributed around $20 on Kickstarter, Enda offered a referral rewards programme, incentives and discounts to buyers who ordered more than one pair to increase contributions. Were they to do it again, Osembo says they would run the campaign for longer and promote it with live events.

Selling shoes on pre-order bought them time. Orders began coming in from June 2016 and had a six-month delivery deadline but in the end, the first shoes weren't shipped before July 2017. This was because the shoe manufacturer wanted a minimum order of 10 000 pairs, while Osembo and Kennedy only had orders for 2 000, which meant they had to find a new supplier.

Osembo says Enda's future lies in e-commerce. She intends

to keep most of the sales online to reduce operating costs and maintain a direct relationship with their customers.

When it comes to managing Enda's finances on a day-to-day basis, Osembo says, "We try to break down our operations to manage the supply chain between ordering and receiving raw materials. It allows us to manage the time that money is tied up in stock."

Osembo admits that, like any cash-strapped start-up, Enda seeks investors. "At the moment Enda is operating lean and we don't have money to pay ourselves." Yet their approach to seeking investment has changed as the company matured. "In the beginning we spent a lot of time and energy knocking on doors that didn't open. It was exhausting. We could have achieved much more had we knocked on doors which were specifically looking for people like us. It's better to approach investors who are a good fit for you."

MANUFACTURING A RUNNING SHOE

Enda originally wanted to manufacture its shoes entirely in Kenya. However, financial constraints and the manufacturing sector's lack of capacity forced them to turn to Chinese manufacturers who would accept their small production order and allow them to keep the price at KSh10 000 (around $100) a pair.

Finding a supplier thousands of kilometres away was difficult. "We established partnerships in China based on referrals because it's harder to let down someone you know than a stranger," says Osembo.

However, manufacturing outside of Kenya still proved a sobering business lesson in the art of trust and navigating language barriers. Their second production of 6 000 pairs expe-

rienced quality issues. As it's not possible to check each shipment shoe by shoe, the defects were discovered only on arrival
in East Africa. To avoid such challenges, Enda is diversifying
its supply chain; if one factory experiences a manufacturing
fault, another can take over production to ensure deliverables
stay on schedule.

The imported shoe components are assembled in a factory
in Mtwapa, northeast of the Kenyan port city Mombasa, which
employs 18 people on the production line. While Enda's supply
chain is divided between Kenya and China, their aim is to
make it a 100 per cent Kenyan-produced brand in the next three
years.

Their 2017 runners' survey showed that their customers are
determined to reduce waste. More than three-quarters of the
respondents supported Enda's use of newspaper as packing
material rather than new or upcycled materials. In line with this
and the growing demand for ethically produced clothing, Enda
is working on a long-term plan to create environmentally sus-
tainable products from recycled materials.

The company is socially responsible, too. Giving is part of
its DNA and Enda wants to help surrounding communities to
grow as it grows. Through the Enda Community Foundation, it
donates two per cent of revenue to social causes that champion
women, youth and differently-abled people.

Despite the success of the Kickstarter campaign, it also
brought unexpected challenges. Distributing the shoes to 32
countries proved a logistical nightmare. Couriers were expensive, there were additional costs based on package size rather
than weight, and customers had to pay import duties upon
delivery.

As a result, Enda now focuses solely on its biggest markets

– Kenya, the United States and Australia – rather than pursuing global growth to the detriment of service quality. "When we expand, we want to do it right," says Osembo. Ultimately, the plan is to distribute across Africa, the European Union and South America. "For now, our biggest obsession is customer service. We are working to be better. Being mindful of our customer guides us."

EMBRACING CO-CREATION

Despite downsizing its market, Enda has increased its product range. "We started as a product company and evolved into a brand company." By engaging with customers online – through Medium, LinkedIn and social media – Enda is prototyping products its target market wants. "Transforming into a brand has allowed us to diversify into apparel and accessories, such as running gear and bracelets," says Osembo. "If we had been set on producing shoes only, we would not have expanded as quickly."

Enda's annual runners' survey provides insights into customers' needs, running styles, motivations and brand loyalty. It forced Osembo and Kennedy back to the drawing board when they learnt that although 15 per cent of their first batch of shoes were bought by Kenyans, the price was too high for the local market. Now they are working on more affordable shoes as well as a second design, code-named HMT (high mileage trainer), for long-distance runs or marathons.

Well-targeted, good social media content is the best marketing solution for SMEs with limited resources, says Osembo. "Social media is changing the game. It has levelled the playing field for small businesses. Focus on your key strengths. Don't compare yourself to a more established brand. Focus on your identity and what makes you unique, then shout it from the rooftops.

"Our social media stories allow us to reach potential customers across borders. My advice to small companies is to create content that resonates with people. We tell stories from a Kenyan perspective. Enda uses social media to talk about coaching, diet, training and resting. We have become a valuable reference for running information and have created an online community," she says. "People call us the Kenyan running guys."

She stresses the importance of being authentic and honest when telling your story. "Tell the story of how you began, your business journey, admit to your challenges and business lessons. It will resonate with customers, allow them to connect with your brand and encourage empathy. People care about us and we care about them. We have a relationship with our customers rather than transactions."

A LABOUR OF LOVE

The Enda journey has taught Osembo that while things will never be perfect, it's vital to keep trying. "It's about that nth time, when you are tired and have done the same thing a million times. Then, one day, it all falls into place," she says.

But if it's not for you, it's not for you. She believes that not everyone is cut out to be an entrepreneur and says not everyone has to be one either. "Some people are financial analysts or artists. We don't all have to be the same." Nor do entrepreneurs have to succumb to the public perception that they have to sacrifice everything. She emphasises the need to prioritise your wellbeing. "Even runners have at least one rest day a week to give their muscles time to repair themselves. Make healthy and conscious decisions. Look after yourself because your body has a limit. A healthy state of mind will help you to formulate better ideas. You cannot do that if you are not eating, sleeping and exercising.

"Always be cognisant of the difference between quantity and quality. They are two different things. There is hard work and then there is smart work. Working 80 hours a week doesn't mean you will make lots of money. While someone else may be working much less, they may be better at addressing the key drivers and core entities of their business."

The ongoing support of a competent team that functions independently of the owner is vital for this. "You have a much better chance of building a company with a team which challenges you rather than agreeing with everything you say or do. If my team disagrees with me, I want them to tell me rather than say, 'The boss said so, so that is what we're going to do.'"

Being the mother of two small children taught her that, just as a parent celebrates a child's milestones, so entrepreneurs should celebrate their successes, remain motivated and keep the end goal in sight instead of constantly moving from one challenge to the next. "I consider Enda one of my children. I have to protect it and let it crawl before it can walk. It has been a labour of love. As I raise my kids, I see the parallels. A start-up is a growing child that you must nurture and protect at any cost."

Becoming an entrepreneur has also made her more appreciative of her time and aware of how she spends it. "I feel immense guilt when I work late or think about the comfortable and relatively well-paying job I quit in pursuit of my dreams, but then I think of wanting to teach my children that they can be anything they want to be."

While Enda backs a few young and up-and-coming Kenyan athletes, one day Osembo aims to be the official sponsor of Kenya's Olympic athletics team.

"I used to fear that Enda would fail but I don't anymore. We may have a few weaknesses but we can fix them. There is a market for us."

9.

Jean de Dieu Kagabo

Rwandan industrialist always hunting for the next big business idea

By Jaco Maritz

In the late 1990s, when the Rwandan economy was recovering from civil war and the 1994 genocide, Jean de Dieu Kagabo began his journey as an entrepreneur. "Everything was in chaos and the country was rebuilding itself from scratch. People were trying to find themselves again and everyone was trying everything and anything to survive financially," he remembers.

Kagabo had a little money at his disposal and in 1998, when he was 18 years old, he began importing affordable cars, such as Toyota Corollas and Starlets, from Dubai. At first, he only brought in one or two vehicles at a time, making a few hundred dollars profit on each, and over time gradually grew the venture. Still, there were times he couldn't afford the import taxes and left vehicles at customs while he looked for buyers. "If a client liked the car, they would pay me an advance which I used to pay the taxes so that I could deliver the car."

Importing vehicles was, however, not generating much money and Kagabo saw it as no more than a way to make ends meet and save until he was able to invest in something more lucrative. This turned out to be a fuel station. He rented premises and bought fuel from Rwandan suppliers. But once the country began to stabilise, international fuel companies such as Shell entered the market and pushed out small dealers such as Kagabo.

That dark cloud had a silver lining as the same multinationals needed truck owners to transport fuel to their service stations across the country. Based on the good relationship he had with the banks because of his previous business dealings, Kagabo secured a loan to buy a truck and began transporting fuel. This, too, didn't last long as the companies eventually began operating their own fleets of trucks.

Having a truck, Kagabo went looking for other companies that needed transport services and, in 2002, landed a contract with logistics operator SDV Transami (now Bolloré Africa Logistics) in neighbouring Uganda. It was his job to transport goods between the Ugandan capital Kampala and Sudan – it was a difficult route with bad roads and security problems. Kagabo didn't do any driving himself; he managed the business from a small apartment in Kampala and employed drivers.

After a few years, Kagabo left Uganda and returned, with his truck, to Rwanda in 2005. He had made some money with his transport business and went in search of his next venture.

FINDING INSPIRATION IN CHINA

In the early 2000s, the Chinese economy was booming with average annual growth rates of 10 per cent. Kagabo was intrigued by this new El Dorado and wanted to go and see it for himself.

He flew to Guangzhou, a sprawling port city and one of China's major trade and commercial hubs. On his own and unable to speak the local language, Kagabo was overwhelmed by the millions of people and the fast pace after coming from laid-back Rwanda.

He didn't have a concrete plan for what he was going to do in China, but in the back of his mind he hoped to stumble upon an opportunity to sell a product from Africa to the over one billion Chinese. "When I got there it was a different story. I couldn't pinpoint a single product they didn't already have," he recalls.

A visit to the Canton Fair, one of China's largest and oldest trade shows attended by manufacturers from across the country, steered Kagabo into a new direction when he came across a machine for making toilet paper. It was something that Rwandans needed: "We are one of the poorest countries in Africa. So I was looking for a basic mass-market product, nothing fancy. What is one of the most basic human needs after food and medicine? It is hygiene. Toilet paper is something people use every day."

Kagabo built his business case on the fact that most of the toilet paper available in landlocked Rwanda was imported from neighbouring countries via road, which greatly inflated prices. If he could manufacture it in Rwanda, he could sell it at half the price of the imported brands. Although there was another domestic toilet paper manufacturer at the time, the company didn't have the capacity to supply the entire market. Furthermore, Kagabo saw potential to export to neighbouring Democratic Republic of the Congo (DRC) and Burundi.

He returned to Rwanda, sold his truck to free up some capital, and went back to China to buy the machine. All he then needed was money to buy the first batch of raw materials.

Again, Kagabo had a plan. In China he had come across a company that produced trailers for transporting shipping containers by road. He knew such trailers were expensive in

Rwanda and that transport companies often had to wait a long time for an order to be delivered. Leveraging his industry contacts, he connected the Chinese manufacturer with a Rwandan company, which placed an order for six trailers. The commission from the transaction allowed him to buy the raw materials he needed.

BECOMING AN INDUSTRIALIST

In 2007, 27-year-old Kagabo set up shop in a small factory in the capital, Kigali, and named his company Soft Group. He doesn't find it strange that he was buying machinery from China and establishing himself as an industrialist at an age when many young people are still finding themselves. "You can never be too young to make money. Age is just a number when it comes to business," he says.

Soft Group did not make a profit immediately and Kagabo describes those early days as hard. He had to train a team which had no previous manufacturing or production experience. "It is difficult to train and manage people in a country that never really had much of a manufacturing sector. Everything was new to our workers."

He also soon discovered that having a better product at a lower price wasn't a guarantee of shelf space in shops. His brand was unknown in the market. Kagabo went to corner shops and markets stalls and arranged deals that allowed shopkeepers to stock the toilet paper and pay him only once it has been sold. "It was tough, really tough, to introduce a new product in a small market like Rwanda where everyone was accustomed to one brand," he says.

Being in a small country also had its advantages, though. Once people began buying his toilet rolls, word spread quickly.

Within about six months, shopkeepers and wholesalers began to approach *him*.

With the toilet-paper business still in its baby shoes, Kagabo wanted to diversify and began to make detergents. This, he now admits, was a mistake. The detergents sold well but Kagabo didn't fully appreciate how expensive the imported raw materials would be. It forced him to dip into the money intended for the toilet paper side of the business, which meant his original product suffered.

With 20/20 hindsight, he says that when developing a business plan for a particular product, entrepreneurs need to have a clear idea of the size of the market they are targeting. And if that opportunity is large enough, it is important to stick with that one product until it can stand on its own feet before branching out. "Focus on one thing until it can sustain itself. Luckily I discovered this at a young age, so I stopped with the detergents, and focused on the toilet paper."

It didn't take him long to spot another opportunity: plastic drinking straws. In certain parts of Rwanda it is traditional to share banana beer (*urwagwa*) in a wooden container (*umuvure*) with a shared reusable natural straw. For hygienic reasons, the government banned these straws. "I saw it as an opportunity. We were the first factory in Rwanda to produce single-use drinking straws," says Kagabo.

Since 2014, Kagabo operates from a much larger factory in Kigali's Special Economic Zone and now employs over 200 people. He has branched out and currently makes several other products. One of the most popular is biodegradable woven sacks used by farmers for their produce. He runs this part of the business as a separate company called Soft Packaging which was established in the same year that they moved premises. He is also involved in plastics recycling and manufactures items such as plastic sheeting for the construction industry and greenhouse covers.

One of the biggest hurdles to expand his companies is access to affordable financing as the interest rates charged by banks currently average around 17 per cent. "The market is there and it is growing but we still face a challenge in terms of borrowing money for the expansion of the business," he says.

DOING BUSINESS IN A COUNTRY WITH BIG AMBITIONS

Rwanda is often referred to as the Singapore of Africa, an analogy most visitors to Kigali would agree with. It is efficient, orderly and clean. Rwanda has transformed itself into one of the continent's most business-friendly countries. It is placed second in sub-Saharan Africa (and 41st globally) on the World Bank's Doing Business rankings for 2018 and is the region's third most competitive economy, according to the World Economic Forum's 2017-2018 Global Competitiveness Index. The economy has grown rapidly, expanding by an average of 7.5 per cent between 2008 and 2017.

Despite the impressive economic figures and reforms, a large percentage of the population still lives in extreme poverty. Rwanda also has a number of drawbacks for businesses: the population is small at about 12 million, the country has few natural resources and no sea port. The government has prioritised a number of areas where it believes Rwanda has a competitive advantage, which include the knowledge economy, information and communications technology (ICT), financial innovation, light manufacturing and intraregional trade.

Kagabo's companies are benefitting from the state's drive to boost the manufacturing sector. The Kigali Special Economic

Zone is geared to make life easier for manufacturers by providing serviced commercial land, reliable and cheaper electricity, and by having less red tape. "The industrial area has many benefits, number one being stable electricity. In plastics manufacturing, an interruption of one second in the production line can lead to big losses. The zone has its own dedicated power supply, as well as backup generators," he explains.

The Rwanda Development Board, which is modelled on Singapore's Economic Development Board to promote business and investment, encourages prospective investors to think bigger than the domestic market. Because of Rwanda's location, it is an ideal base from which to export to Burundi, the DRC, Tanzania and Uganda. Rwanda is also part of the East African Community, which gives it preferential trade access to a market of 170 million people.

Kagabo has tapped into these cross-border opportunities by exporting to the eastern DRC and southern Uganda. He has a small depot close to the DRC border that carries all his companies' products. "We have a marketer in the DRC and, when we sign a client there, we export the products from that depot, or they simply come across the border and buy it themselves," he adds.

However, doing business in eastern DRC, which has suffered from years of instability, is much different from the orderly way things are done in Rwanda. Kagabo says the biggest obstacle in the DRC is the ever-changing regulations, particularly regarding import taxes.

FROM SPARKLING WINE TO SOCKS TO...

Kagabo still travels to China regularly and attends industry shows such as Chinaplas, one of the world's biggest plastics trade fairs, to keep abreast of the latest machinery and make new connections.

In a sideline venture, he and a partner are the Rwandan distributors of Luc Belaire, the French sparkling wine known for partnering with American rappers such as Rick Ross and Young Thug. They approached the company's regional representative in Dubai and have been selling the drink in Rwanda ever since.

The demand for high-end alcohol is partly driven by the tourism and conference industries, which the government actively promotes. The Kigali Convention Centre, which was completed in 2016, has played host to large events such as the African Green Revolution Forum, the Afreximbank annual general meeting and the Africa Health Forum. International hotel chains such as Marriott and Radisson Blu have also opened in the capital. "There are people coming here who want to be able to enjoy what they are consuming in other countries," says Kagabo.

Still, he is always thinking what next; for instance, clothing and textile manufacturing. Throughout East Africa, much of the clothes sold at markets are second-hand imports from the West. In 2016, when Rwanda introduced a 12-fold tariff increase on second-hand clothing to stimulate local production, it attracted the ire of the United States, which retaliated by revoking Rwanda's African Growth and Opportunity Act privilege to export clothing duty-free to America. "When people see something as a problem, I always see it as an opportunity," says Kagabo. He is thinking socks and underwear. "People wear them every day and you have to wash it every day. You can't wear it twice."

Another of his business ideas is for a simple but widely used item: matches. Every Rwandan household, whether lower or upper class, uses matches. Yet matches are still being imported despite being easy to make. "No one has done it."

Then there's Rwanda's goal to provide electricity access to the whole country by 2024. "What do we need for this? We need electric cables. There isn't a factory making cables in Rwanda."

Despite all he has achieved, Kagabo, currently 38, doesn't feel like he has arrived. "I can't say I'm there yet. I still have a long journey to go because my country is growing and the region is growing. The sky is the limit."

10.

Addis Alemayehou

Serial entrepreneur bringing the world to Ethiopia

By Jaco Maritz

Partner, managing partner, board member, senior advisor ... the list of positions Addis Alemayehou holds concurrently is impressive. Many of these roles are at his own companies, which include one of Ethiopia's biggest advertising agencies, a popular television channel and a telecommunications start-up in South Africa. Yet Addis comes across as pretty calm and collected. He admits that on the inside, though, the pressure often gets to him.

"There are nights I don't sleep and there have been times where the stress has threatened my health. Things don't always work out the way you want them to, or the numbers don't come in the way you expected, or clients have an issue with your service. It is a never-ending rollercoaster but it is part of being an entrepreneur," says the 47-year-old Addis.

In 1980, when Addis was a young boy, his family relocated to Nairobi, Kenya, to escape Ethiopia's then socialist government. At 16, his parents sent him to North Dakota in the United States where he completed his last year of schooling. After living in the States for a year and a half, Addis moved to Canada to join his family who had since emigrated there. He enrolled at the University of Toronto but ended up studying for only about a year, opting instead to work a variety of odd jobs and to pursue his business ambitions.

It was in Canada that Addis started his first entrepreneurial venture: buying and leasing properties. "I bought my first real estate when I was 18 and by the time I was 21, I owned three properties. When the Toronto real estate market crashed in 1989, guys like me could afford to buy property. There was a huge immigrant community coming into the city, particularly Somalis, and they needed a place to stay."

In the late 1990s, while still living in Canada, Addis began researching Africa's mobile telecommunications industry, which was still in its infancy. At the time, several international mobile network operators were looking to acquire operating licences in Africa. Sensing an opportunity, he submitted a proposal to South African mobile operators MTN and Vodacom to partner with him to acquire a licence in Ethiopia. "I had no clue how a licence would work, but I was 29 and just anxious to get back home to Ethiopia to do something."

Vodacom was interested, and invited Addis and the partners he had assembled for a meeting in South Africa. "I was crazy nervous. It was my first boardroom meeting. I called my brother-in-law and said: 'Man, I don't know if I can do this. My hands are sweating.' I'll never forgot what he told me: 'They are not going to beat you up. They can just say no. The worst that can happen is that they don't like the deal. They will say no, and then they will say thank you and goodbye – what do you have to lose?'"

Although Vodacom signed a memorandum of understanding with Addis after the meeting, nothing came of the deal, as the Ethiopian government didn't allow any mobile operator besides the state-owned Ethio Telecom into the country. It wasn't before 2018 that the government for the first time indicated its intent to open the telecoms industry to private investors.

"We had a few contacts in Ethiopia and, being inexperienced, we simply assumed that if we came in with a company such as Vodacom willing to invest hundreds of millions of dollars, the Ethiopian government would welcome us with open arms," he says. "It was obviously not the case."

These days, obtaining a mobile network licence in almost any African country is costly and requires high-level negotiations. It certainly is not something one would expect an inexperienced 20-something to attempt. But Addis looks at the experience as a learning curve. "Sometimes being young and clueless is good because you learn things as you go, rather than sitting behind a desk and reading about it. It taught me the basic things: how to dress, how to shake someone's hand at a corporate meeting, how to put together a pitch document.

"For me, it's always about finding a gap and an opportunity I can exploit. At the time, the opportunity was to get into mobile in one of the biggest countries on the continent. It didn't work out but at least it got me back home so that I could look at the next opportunity."

After abandoning his mobile licence plans, in 2003, Addis began working at the United States Agency for International Development (USAID) in Ethiopia. The American government had just introduced the African Growth and Opportunity Act (AGOA), which allowed qualifying African countries to export a wide range of products to the United States duty-free. It was Addis's responsibility to find Ethiopian companies which had products ready for export and connect them with buyers in the States.

His five-year stint at USAID was a deep dive into the Ethiopian economy and served him well to this day. Addis says, "It was the ideal opportunity to learn how local businesses operate. The job also allowed me to work with the Ethiopian ministries of trade and industry and learn how government works. Furthermore, it gave me insight into what the donor world is all about. I began to understand Ethiopia on a different level without having to spend my own resources to do it."

LAUNCHING ETHIOPIA'S FIRST ENGLISH RADIO STATION

While working with USAID, Addis frequently travelled to Nairobi where he still had many contacts because he grew up there. During one such trip he asked his friend, Chris Kirubi – a well-known Kenyan businessman with interests in property, insurance, media and manufacturing – which one of his investments he enjoys the most. Capital FM, replied Kirubi, his radio station.

That got Addis thinking about doing something similar in Ethiopia. "I convinced Chris to let me spend a week at Capital FM with him and his management team. I sat in on every meeting, listened to advertising sales calls, observed the DJs and spent time with the tech guys. I came to the conclusion that there was an opportunity to do this in Ethiopia as there wasn't a single English FM radio station in Addis Ababa."

Back home, Addis applied for a licence to operate a radio station. He convinced the regulators by stressing that Addis Ababa, the home of the African Union, was one of the world's largest diplomatic capitals with many English-speaking residents and visitors – a group that couldn't be ignored.

In 2008, he received a licence and called his station Afro FM. The business made money from advertisers, which were keen to market to the affluent expats the station was targeting.

HELPING MULTINATIONALS MARKET THEMSELVES

Ethiopia, a country synonymous with famine in the 1980s, has made significant economic progress. In the decade between 2000 and 2009, its economy grew by an average of 8.5 per cent every year. This, coupled with a large population (about 95 million today), attracted the interest of multinational companies and brands.

Having already had some experience with the advertising industry through the radio station, Addis saw potential in catering for the marketing and communication needs of these companies. Therefore, in 2011, he launched the advertising, branding and public relations agency 251 Communications. (251 is Ethiopia's international dialling code.)

"Although the government still didn't allow foreign investment in a range of sectors, we already had the likes of Coca-Cola, PepsiCo and Tiger Brands in the country. Ethiopia was moving away from a communist business environment to one that would attract more big international brands. We certainly have a population size that excites consumer brands. I anticipated that sooner or later, these multinationals were going to start spending some serious money on advertising," he explains.

251 Communications today employs over 40 full-time staff and counts Pfizer, The Coca-Cola Company, DHL and the Bill & Melinda Gates Foundation among its clients. But when it first opened its doors, the staff consisted only of Addis, his business partner and a few interns. They counted their pennies.

"We had a tiny one-room office. We had the furniture made rather than buying it. We had used-laptops because we couldn't afford new ones. We started on a very tight budget.

"I see many entrepreneurs who over-invest without really looking at the market and the returns on their investment. You should put in only what you need to start and gradually put in more money as you grow. Nobody starts off earning revenue on the first day. Getting your business up and running is where you should spend your energy and resources, not on nice furniture and a nice office," says Addis.

With few competitors in the market, 251 Communications landed Heineken – which at the time had just bought two state-owned breweries from the Ethiopian government – as its first client. The first time Heineken came to see them, they used a friend's office next door. "The lesson here is that you can overcome any hurdle. When we met with the Heineken marketing manager, I was dead honest. I said, 'We're new, we're just starting up, we're hungry, we will do whatever it takes to make you successful. Please stick with us.' And they did."

To further capitalise on growing international interest in the continent, Addis, in 2013, co-founded PR company Africa Communications Media Group (ACG) with his friend Mimi Kalinda. "ACG was set up because we had a lot of multinational PR firms from the European Union and the United States looking at doing work in Africa and not really getting the gist of what the different markets need in terms of local insight," he explains. ACG operates from Johannesburg and its clients include MTN and Dalberg.

SWAPPING RADIO FOR TV

Addis sold his stake in Afro FM right after starting 251 Communications but kept exploring possibilities in broadcasting. Initially he wanted to launch MTV Ethiopia but after a meeting with MTV in South Africa, they declined. MTV did not believe the channel would generate enough advertising revenue to cover the licensing cost and operational expenses. The MTV representative told him, "If I were you, I would start my own channel."

Addis and his partner went back to the drawing board and researched the Ethiopian television market. They found that most Ethiopians who have TVs also have satellite dishes to watch free satellite channels such as ArabSat which broadcasts throughout the Middle East and parts of Africa. However, these shows were only in Arabic or English, not in the local Amharic language. Many Ethiopian children have even learnt to speak Arabic because of ArabSat.

"We felt if we brought that same content to the Ethiopian market in Amharic, a language which people understand, that it would do well."

Addis and his partner formed Kana TV in 2015 and teamed up with Moby Group, a television and radio broadcasting company founded in Afghanistan with operations throughout south and central Asia and the Middle East. In the beginning, most of the programmes were international television dramas, such as the Turkish series *Kara Para Aşk* and Indian soap opera *Saraswatichandra*, which had been dubbed into Amharic. Although much of the content is still dubbed, Kana TV now also produces original programmes like an Ethiopian music and entertainment show as well as a regular news insert.

It took Kana TV two years to break even – it earns most of its revenue through advertising – and it currently commands around 40 per cent of Ethiopia's prime-time market. It has been so popular that some conservative voices have even blamed Kana TV for corrupting traditional Ethiopian values.

PARTNERING FOR SUCCESS

Addis has built most of his ventures by identifying a gap in the market and then partnering with companies that have the necessary technical expertise. And in a few instances, he has simply copied and pasted successful international business models. In all his businesses, though, he is very hands-off, and says, "I'm usually the guy who comes up with the idea and puts the team together. The rest of the time I'm a shareholder who spends maybe 20 per cent of my time on each entity.

"It takes a bit of management and discipline, which I'm still trying to learn, but it has worked out. That is how I see my role, rather than being pinned down to one company."

The trick, he says, is to work with the right partners. "For me, the number one thing is to pick the right people to work with, because they will take the burden off your shoulders and share the risk and stress. "I always look for a partner who has something I don't have. For instance, I'm good in the marketing and strategy space, but I'm not good at numbers. With Kana, I didn't know anything about the technical aspects of running a TV station or about production. If you are just going to add more of the resources you already have, why look for a partner?"

Addis again employed this partnership strategy for one of his latest businesses, called Arada Mobile, which offers preferential call-home rates and Ethiopian digital content to the hundreds of thousands of Ethiopians living in South Africa. "I needed local expertise, so I have a partner who has lived in

South Africa for 16 years and understands the Ethiopian community there and knows how to talk and market to them."

THE REAL OPPORTUNITIES ARE YET TO COME

Until early 2018, Ethiopia experienced years of massive anti-government protests and violence driven by the Oromo and Amhara ethnic groups which felt marginalised by the government. Economically, the country also suffers from large unemployment and a shortage of foreign currency. However, its new Prime Minister, the 42-year-old Abiy Ahmed – who came to power in April 2018 after the unexpected resignation of Hailemariam Desalegn – has introduced several reforms that have made people excited about Ethiopia's future again. Abiy is the country's first Oromo leader and out of the blocks got rid of controversial government officials, lifted media and internet bans, freed political prisoners, announced his intention to open state-owned companies to outside investment and made peace with neighbouring Eritrea, putting an end to the 20-year war between the two countries.

At the end of July 2018, Abiy made his first official visit to the United States where he implored the large Ethiopian community there to invest in their home country. Addis was particularly excited by this as 251 Communications had already begun working on a real estate expo in December 2018, when large numbers of the Ethiopian diaspora will be in the country for Christmas.

"For the majority of Ethiopians living abroad, their first investment in the country is property. I had many friends and family who were enquiring about property in Addis and Ethiopia, and I found myself spending a lot of time calling and enquiring about who was selling and which real estate company is reputable. I realised there is probably a lot of people facing the same issue, and felt bringing all the real estate companies under one roof would be an ideal way to service the public. It is an opportunity I saw and ran with," says Addis.

"I have always followed my gut, but I have also been lucky," he notes. "Businesses did not enter Ethiopia in 2001, it was a crazy thing to do. Nobody launched an English FM station at the time. Even Kana TV was risky, if I have to be honest, Ethiopians could have rejected it. Luckily they didn't. Now we are experiencing a fairly exciting time because it is possible to adopt what has worked elsewhere and bring it to Ethiopia.

"There is a lot more to do, not just in Ethiopia, but elsewhere on the continent, too. I think we have not even scratched the surface as far as opportunities in Africa go."

11.

Kasope Ladipo-Ajai
Nigerian cooking made convenient

By Jeanette Clark

Food is essential to the Nigerian way of life. The country boasts a smorgasbord of spices and spice mixes which are distinctive to its cuisine and used in traditional dishes such as Banga rice, yam porridge, the mighty jollof rice (lovingly called 'party rice') and Ayamase or ofada rice. These are only some of the dishes enjoyed by the country's more than 300 ethnic groups on a regular basis.

When Kasope Ladipo-Ajai and Olatayo, her husband, travelled the world, they missed the comfort food of home. Even when searching African stores in the countries they had visited, they could never find Nigerian-produced spices or products on the shelves. Upon enquiry, it turned out that issues with packaging and international certification standards were the reasons for the lack of original Nigerian food products. This bothered Ladipo-Ajai.

"Let's not lie. Nigeria is a very big African country and we make up a large percentage of the African diaspora. Why could I not find Nigerian ingredients?" she asks. To her, the gap in the market was glaringly obvious; there was an opportunity to bring Nigerian food to the diaspora, and the world.

Thus, in 2012, Ladipo-Ajai and Olatayo founded OmoAlata, a small Nigerian food processing and services company.

Convenience is also one of the company's major selling points. Preparing traditional Nigerian dishes is extremely time-consuming: from finding tomatoes, onions and peppers at the market to combining the pepper-spice mix and simmering the stew for hours on end to achieve the correct consistency for the sauce. OmoAlata – translated from Yoruba, it means *son or daughter of a spice seller* – solves that problem by providing ready-made soups, spices and pepper sauces made from organic ingredients.

NOT A TYPICAL START

Conventional wisdom advocates that aspiring businesspeople should find their passion, and then follow it. For Ladipo-Ajai it was the other way around and passion did not precede opportunity. "To be honest, the opportunity came first for us. The passion for this business only came later," she admits.

When she tells of her upbringing and her mother and father's parenting style, she refers to both as unconventional for the time and place. "I grew up in Ibadan, a smaller city than Lagos. My parents were quite liberal – they believed in allowing us to voice our thoughts, to be free with adults. I could tell my dad what I was thinking and dreaming about and he would always encourage me." It is this support from her researcher-father and teacher-mother that Ladipo-Ajai believes steered her towards becoming an entrepreneur.

Today, "fail fast" is a mantra-like term that has been popularised by the Silicon Valley-culture of accepting repeated failure as building blocks for future success, but Ladipo-Ajai already learnt this principle as a child. "My parents didn't limit us in our dreaming. They encouraged us. We were never taught that failing is a problem. If you fail, you just moved on to the next thing. Today, my two siblings are entrepreneurs, too," she says.

A RECIPE FOR SUCCESS

After six years at the head of operations, Ladipo-Ajai openly admits that it hasn't always been easy. In the beginning, the couple had to use their personal savings to fund OmoAlata and had to stretch the money as far as possible. To this day, her greatest fear is that all the years of hard work and sacrifice won't pay off.

"I can't allow myself to believe that it could happen, though. The only way that will happen is if I give up," she says. Before departing on her OmoAlata journey, Ladipo-Ajai had put her BSc degree in computer science from Babcock University in Nigeria to use as an IT business support analyst for airline Virgin Nigeria. "I could have stayed an analyst and know I would have progressed up the ladder. If I therefore give up now, it would mean that I have wasted all these years. It is one of the things that makes me stay the course. You have to make it happen. You can never give up!"

It doesn't mean that she is uncomfortable with the sacrifices she has had to make, as they were made by choice. "I don't have regrets. I know where I want to be," she says. She credits this tenacity for landing the job at airline Virgin Nigeria. When asked the usual question of where she sees herself in five years, she replied that she would not be working for them anymore – she would most likely be running her own business. It made her interviewers chuckle but they hired her anyway. Five years later, OmoAlata was established.

In fact, Ladipo-Ajai advises anyone wanting to venture out on their own to first gain experience at an established company. "If someone has the opportunity to work in a structured, formal environment, they should definitely do that first. I do not believe my time at Virgin Nigeria was wasted. You have to learn the business of business before striking out."

She believes it is just as important to "start by learning". The two co-founders knew absolutely nothing about the food processing business when they started OmoAlata. "For the first six to eight months, we only did research. We spoke to caterers, we gave out free samples to family and friends. It was a long process," she says. "We also had to learn what kind of packaging to use, which certifications – for instance, from the Nigerian National Agency for Food and Drug Administration and Control (NAFDAC) – were needed."

Then came their first sale, a relatively small order for 20 packets from one shop. They kept their offering simple and stuck to only one product for almost four years. "We started with the pepper mix; we had to gain people's confidence. We knew that eventually we would add more niche products, but this particular mix is one thing that is used throughout all of Nigeria; on average a Nigerian would eat it at least once a day," she explains. After adding ofada sauce as their second product in 2016, it quickly became the top seller.

While many entrepreneurs go it alone, Ladipo-Ajai believes her business partnership with her husband adds to the company's success, especially in the Nigerian business context. "When you pitch for funding or new business, one of the first things people ask is whether your business is a partnership or a solo operation." She believes investors and backers like to know that a business does not depend on only one person's energy. In a successful partnership, the two people push and drive each other, helping the business through the difficult times it is bound to encounter. "It is important to have a partner but most importantly, you have to really make sure you have the right one," she says. In their case, their differences and disagreements often lead to even better ideas.

FINDING TRACTION

OmoAlata's first breakthrough came when the company received NAFDAC certification. Without it, Ladipo-Ajai says, bigger retail stores in Nigeria will definitely not sign on your product. Once its products had it, more sales materialised. OmoAlata is currently stocked by 17 retailers.

Shortly after receiving their NAFDAC certification, they redesigned OmaAlata's packaging to be more recognisable, which resulted in a further increase in sales.

The company had another boost when Ladipo-Ajai won the 2015 She Leads Africa (SLA) entrepreneurship showcase. The SLA organisation has a presence in several African countries and offers engaging online content and hosts pan-African events such as the showcase. "It brought much-needed publicity for the company at a time when we were ready for it," Ladipo-Ajai says.

"It is hard doing business in Nigeria. Quite a lot of the smaller, local stores struggle and shut down," Ladipo-Ajai says of the fluctuating number of retail outlets available to OmoAlata. "It goes up and down. At one point, we had 40 stores selling our products. Then it went down to 20 before going up to 25, only to drop again."

In addition to retailers, they also supply a popular Nigerian online store and sell wholesale to restaurants and caterers too.

At the moment, online sales are growing faster than the other two channels but she knows that the business can stay afloat only if the wholesale side of it is going well. "My business is about numbers. Our profit margins are low and unless I sell in bulk, the bottom line does not make sense."

OmoAlata's production is done at their factory in Lagos, where the staff complement has grown from two in 2012 to 11 in 2018. Since mid-2016, it has been able to ramp up capacity to 5 000 items a month but current production is standing at half that figure. The company is poised and ready for growth, and Ladipo-Ajai is aggressively looking for the opportunities that will get it there.

Outsourcing distribution and marketing is one option Ladipo-Ajai is considering. Until now, the company has mostly relied on word of mouth, customer-driven exposure on social media and working through membership organisations it belongs to. Entrusting this function to a third party will allow them to focus on the production side, which is OmoAlata's core competency.

While most of OmoAlata's sales are generated in Nigeria, Ladipo-Ajai travelled to the United States in June and again in August 2018 and is in negotiations with potential importers. She is hopeful that these meetings with lead to full-scale sales in America and Canada by the end of 2018.

UNIQUELY NIGERIAN CHALLENGES

Ask Ladipo-Ajai about doing business in Nigeria and she replies that the going gets tough – often. When setting up the factory, for example, they had to deal with inconsistent power supply.

"This is one of the biggest challenges for any Nigerian business, especially those trading in perishable products," she says. "Supplying your own power is not an option as it increases overheads too much and makes it impossible for small companies to survive." OmoAlata therefore found ways to work around the unreliable electricity in the factory but moved the refrigerated storage facility to a residential area where power is guaranteed.

Human resources is the second challenge. They found it difficult to hire passionate, dedicated employees and staff turnover is high. "It is very hard to get everyone to understand my dream and not just come to work for the pay. If you find that gem of an employee, you have to take care of them."

Ladipo-Ajai believes it is important to encourage the right culture in her team to be able to build a steady foundation for the next growth phase. "If your HR is not good, no matter what you do, you will fail. Your people are what make your business. You cannot do it alone." She therefore ensures that there is no perceived hierarchy at OmoAlata. "Yes, I am the boss but it does not mean that our employees can't speak their minds."

Another major challenge for smaller businesses in Nigeria, Ladipo-Ajai says, is managing their working capital and structuring payments so that the business remains viable. The reality is that small suppliers like OmoAlata often have to wait long before receiving payment from retailers, which puts cash flow under pressure. "Honestly, the retail stores hold you to ransom. When you are bigger, they won't have a choice but to pay you, but this situation is crippling small businesses."

This is one of the main reasons OmoAlata focuses on business-to-business sales and added an online retail channel.

ENTREPRENEURSHIP NOT FOR THE FAINT-HEARTED

For Ladipo-Ajai, work-life balance is a problematic concept. Being a mother of a baby boy and having to run the day-to-day operations of a growing business in the fast-moving consumer goods sector, the idea makes her laugh. "Some people believe that the ideal is to divide your time 50/50 and everything will then be perfect. The reality is that there is no such thing as perfection, especially if you have a time-consuming business as well as a family," she says. "What is important is to give your best to whatever you're doing at that time and to simply trust that the rest will be fine."

Ladipo-Ajai takes a realistic view of the life she has chosen. She does not romanticise entrepreneurship. "I find it funny that the word 'entrepreneur' seems to be a fad in Nigeria at the moment. I don't want to call myself an entrepreneur because of the notion that it is fantastic to run your own business – you are on Instagram, it's glamorous, blah … blah … Behind the scenes, it is horrible at times. It is not anything like people think.

"From the outside, it might seem wonderful not to have a boss and to be the boss. Many times I work through the night. Often I have to put in my own money because something went wrong. It's not all rosy and nice. It is not for the lily-livered. In a day job, you get paid no matter what. In this world, the boss often does not get paid."

That does not mean she has given up and she still tenaciously believes in the dream behind their company. With the possibility of the North American markets lying in wait and the potential of the Nigerian diaspora totalling millions, Ladipo-Ajai is using her street smarts every day to bring OmoAlata closer to that dream: healthy Nigerian food, without the fuss.

12.

Chijioke Dozie

Leveraging past experiences to disrupt the banking industry

By Jaco Maritz

Many entrepreneurs argue for starting small and not risking too much money in the early stages of a company. But this wasn't the approach of Nigerian businessman Chijioke Dozie. From the outset, he went big by making sizeable investment bets and boldly launching new business concepts.

Together with his brother Ngozi, Dozie founded the financial services firm OneFi, which provides short-term loans through its Paylater mobile app in Nigeria and Ghana. After leaving behind their corporate careers, they have been involved in numerous business ventures. In addition to OneFi, they've launched a chain of coffee shops, tried their hand at fast food restaurants, invested in a Rwandan coffee roaster and backed a Ghanaian fruit juice exporter.

Dozie ascribes his confidence to being raised in an entrepreneurial family and having been exposed to large investment deals while working in the private equity industry early in his career.

"It is always the challenge that motivates us. Frankly, if it is not fun and challenging, I may just as well go and work in a bank or could have stayed with the International Finance Corporation (IFC). I would have had an easy life, travelling the world and attending conferences," he says.

LEARNING THE INVESTMENT GAME

After completing primary school in Nigeria, Dozie attended high school and university in the United Kingdom. His first job was as an investment associate focusing on African operations at the New York-based emerging markets investment company Zephyr Management, which he joined in 2001. There, he got to know the IFC team while working on several investments in which they had partnered with Zephyr. After about two years Dozie moved to the IFC, where he analysed investment opportunities in sub-Saharan Africa.

Both jobs involved working closely with business founders in Africa, which inspired Dozie to join their ranks. He singles out the young founders of pan-African financial services company Bayport, Grant Kurland and Stuart Stone, for having had a particular impact on him.

He met them when Zephyr was considering investing in Bayport. "I was 23 back then and they weren't much older. I was looking at the deal and flying to Zambia and Ghana and examining their business. I was like, 'I want to do what they are doing,'" he recalls.

Dozie resigned from the IFC and, in 2006, enrolled for an MBA at Harvard Business School. Once he'd obtained his MBA, he was ready to head out on his own entrepreneurial path.

He teamed up with his brother to establish investment company Kaizen Venture Partners. Their goal was to invest in distressed companies in Africa while at the same time starting new businesses which have proven successful in other parts of the world but have not yet taken off in the continent.

"In our experience, most African investors and private equity funds want to back healthy companies – businesses that are profitable and probably don't even need the money. But when companies go wrong – when they run into trouble or had a bad year – banks and investors shy away from them despite the fact that they are inherently good businesses. We wanted to invest in such distressed companies," Dozie explains.

The brothers managed to raise $8 million for their investment fund and it wasn't long before they found their first troubled business to invest in: a coffee-roasting company in Rwanda. Their rationale was that Rwandan coffee was of a high quality and in demand internationally.

TAKING A SIP OF THE COFFEE BUSINESS

After turning the Rwandan company around, they began looking at exporting its coffee to new markets, including Nigeria. However, it soon became apparent that there weren't many buyers in Nigeria. This, in turn, made them realise that there was a gap in the Nigerian market for a coffee-restaurant business. In 2012, they opened the first Cafe Neo coffee shop in the upmarket Victoria Island area in Lagos, the country's economic hub.

The location wasn't ideal – the outlet was hidden on the second floor of the building – but the brothers kept it going, despite attracting only a dozen or so customers a day. Nine months later, they secured a counter in an office block housing several international companies. This earned them several loyal customers but the brand still did not take off. Then, in 2014, they decided to take a risk and opened a stand-alone café in a prime yet expensive location. Soon after opening this outlet, Cafe Neo began making a name for itself.

Still, it did not grow as quickly as they had wanted. Coffee is a long-term game in Nigeria and accounts for only a tiny percentage of the hot beverage market, which is dominated by hot chocolate and tea.

The overheads of operating a coffee outlet in Lagos are also astronomical. Because of insufficient and unreliable power supply, businesses often have no choice but to install generators at their own expense. On top of that they need to provide their own water and sanitation. "A 100 square metre outlet could cost $3 000 per month in service charges. That's not even including rent – that's just power, diesel, water and so on. That is a lot of coffee you have to sell. It is actually cheaper for us to open a Cafe Neo store in the United Kingdom than in Nigeria," says Dozie.

They changed tack and began opening smaller outlets in office buildings where most basic services are already available. The guaranteed stream of customers is a plus.

"We don't have as many stand-alone stores anymore because it is just too expensive," he says.

Their goal is to create a low-cost, standardised operation with the potential to scale. The brothers therefore had to resist the urge to make Cafe Neo outlets too frilly. "I can take you to some amazing coffee shops in Lagos that have beautiful art and lovely ornaments. But those places are a labour of love and not something you can replicate over 15 shops. It would be too expensive," explains Dozie.

They have since also appointed a full-time CEO to handle the day-to-day running of the coffee shop business. To simplify its management and to free themselves up, the brothers outsource as much as possible, down to the sandwiches and salads Cafe Neo sells, even though it means having a smaller profit margin.

"I'm a big coffee drinker and I drink coffee there but other than that, we are no longer involved in managing Cafe Neo. We are allowing it to tick over and, once the coffee culture in Nigeria really picks up, we might look at expanding it more aggressively," Dozie says.

RETHINKING FINANCIAL SERVICES

Since meeting the Bayport founders all those years ago, Dozie had been interested in starting a financial services business in Nigeria. It is estimated that well below 10 per cent of the country's population of 196 million have access to credit, while some 61 per cent of the adult population is un- or underbanked.

So, in 2012, around the same time they opened the first Cafe Neo, he and his brother launched the consumer lending company OneFi. The business case was built on the fact that Nigerians struggle to get credit from traditional banks, and even when they do, it still takes weeks for the loans to be approved.

Six years later, OneFi's entire platform is mobile-based but this wasn't always the case. At first, they employed agents who went from one office block to the next and sold loans. Ignoring factors such as an applicant's appearance or their family's standing, OneFi's lending criteria was based largely on the figure at the bottom of their salary slip.

"Because our lending criteria were so formulaic, we could process a loan very quickly. We could process a loan from start to finish and have the money in someone's account within 72 hours," says Dozie.

After a while, using sales agents became restrictive as there is a limit to how many clients they can visit in a day. On top of that, more competitors, many of them unregulated, entered the market as the unsecured lending industry gained traction. These businesses did not always play by the rules and because they didn't properly account for their non-performing loans, they could offer better interest rates. They also poached OneFi's agents, who had been trained at considerable expense.

Unlike their rivals, OneFi has always done everything by the book. From the get-go, they appointed KPMG to audit the business, despite the associated costs. Dozie explains their decision to hire a large auditing firm when the company was still in its infancy: "We wanted to grow by attracting large investors and decided to work with great partners."

After working through agents for three years, OneFi hit the tipping point in 2015 when it raised $20 million in debt and equity from South African payments technology company Net 1 UEPS Technologies. Dozie calls it "a pivotal moment", as it gave them access to capital and "an institutional umbrella".

Even so, he considers financing one of the major challenges faced by Nigerian fintech start-ups. Western venture capital firms typically are hesitant to invest in Nigeria, he says, due to risks such as the volatile currency, which could see the value of an investment drop significantly overnight. Nigerian investors, on the other hand, want the reassurance of a company that is already showing profits.

After taking a long and hard look at their business model, the brothers used Net 1's investment to switch to a digital model. Despite processing loan applications faster than the banks, it had become too capital intensive to physically sign up new customers. "We were basically trying to beat the banks at their own game but we didn't have the funds, we didn't have the systems, and we didn't have the reputation. We saw technology as a way to overcome this," explains Dozie.

They did this through Paylater, an app that works as follows: someone seeking a loan downloads it and submits their personal details and the amount they need, the necessary credit bureau and creditworthiness checks are done instantly and, if approved, the money is deposited into their bank account within five minutes. On the loan's due date, payment is automatically deducted from the customer's bank account.

Before Paylater, OneFi had extended about 9 000 loans per year between 2012 and 2015 through its sales agents. With Paylater, it receives 7 000 applications per day, of which around 2 000 are approved. Because no human intervention is required, the company isn't restricted to Lagos anymore and can handle applications from across the country. By August 2018, Paylater had over 800 000 registered users and had extended loans totalling $17 million since January of that year.

Dozie runs the company as its CEO and focuses mostly on product development and marketing, while Ngozi is CFO and takes care of the financial and data science functions.

GROWING AN APP INTO A BANK

Dozie's vision is to grow OneFi into a fully fledged digital bank with a presence in several African countries. The have already added a fixed-interest investment account to their product list as well as functions that allow users to transfer funds, pay bills and purchase airtime via the Paylater app.

In terms of geographical expansion, OneFi has opened shop in Ghana. But Dozie says the pace of doing business in West Africa is sluggish. "For instance, when we did a deal in Ghana, I wanted to negotiate the agreement over the phone and email, but the other person insisted that I personally come and see him. It meant I had to fly to Ghana for every single discussion."

One of their biggest growth challenges is finding skilled software developers and data scientists, who are in high demand globally by companies with much deeper pockets than OneFi. "People are a huge challenge; it keeps me up at night, and I spend more than 50 per cent of my time looking for staff," Dozie says. He believes one way for tech companies to overcome the skills deficit is to recruit outside Nigeria. For instance, OneFi has data scientists working for them who are based in Cape Town. If it's a choice between having the best talent possible on board and having someone in your office every day, Dozie would go for the first option, every time.

"Of course, a manufacturing business can't have its employees all over the world, but if you are a technology company where everyone doesn't have to be in the same location, you can definitely make it work. I know of businesses that have a CEO in Kenya, a CTO in London and a COO in Johannesburg."

Another challenge has been the fact that the financial services industry is tightly regulated. "What we do is new, and when things are new they sometimes don't fit into the existing regulatory framework." But instead of following the "Uber strategy" of not seeking permission and asking for forgiveness later, OneFi actively works with regulators. "Current regulations don't quite fit what we need but we engage with the regulators and help them to understand our business model. Hopefully we can influence change in this way," Dozie says.

On a personal level, his decision-making has been slowed down by his fear of conflict. He recalls an instance where he identified a talented potential employee who could add considerable value to the company. But because she came with a high salary, there was a real risk that he would have had to let her go if the business didn't take off. Dozie dreaded the thought of having to call her in and to tell her the company could no longer afford her. In the end, he did however take the risk to employ her. "This is an area where I changed considerably over the past year or so. I now embrace conflict by putting myself in tough situations because I need to take those risks. Fear of conflict makes you gun-shy and not as aggressive as you need to be. You have to be fearless to be an entrepreneur. If you are not, you won't operate at your fullest potential."

PRACTISE MAKES PERFECT

"You can't be excellent when you have too many things to focus on. Many entrepreneurs tackle too many opportunities at once, especially in Africa where there are many problems to solve. But everything suffers if you don't focus on one thing."

While he says this with such conviction, it is a lesson Dozie had to learn.

"Day in and day out, my brother and I focus on OneFi, but only after one of our new directors had asked, 'What are you guys doing? I see you on CNN talking about Cafe Neo but then you also have OneFi. You've got to make a choice.' So we did." They are so committed to OneFi that it is difficult to get him to even talk about his interest in Cafe Neo.

An equally important lesson is that all stakeholders in a business transaction must be aligned and have skin in the game if it is to succeed. Dozie learnt this after investing in a troubled company where the owner didn't have the same incentive as his investors to see the business succeed – either way, he was to make money from the deal. "We made the mistake of going into a few such transactions because they were new and exciting, and we had a sort of deal lust. In every single one of those situations we lost money."

After several years in business, Dozie knows how to respond more skilfully when he sees a situation repeating itself. At the investment firm where he worked, he used to look up to his bosses because they could analyse a situation and make a decision in an instant. "I thought they were so clever and that I'd never be like them." Now he knows that they weren't necessarily smarter than him but that they had just seen it all before.

Dozie too now has the benefit of experience and says, "Sometimes my brother and I would be in a meeting with our team and they'd be enthusiastic about an opportunity that looks amazing from the outside. When we say, 'No', they usually respond, 'What the hell?' But it's because we'd seen that type of person or situation before and remember getting completely screwed.

"It sounds crazy, but you almost have to lose money before you can make money."

13.

Sylvester Chauke

Marketer with a passion to take African brands global

By Jaco Maritz

Sylvester Chauke first made a name for himself as national marketing manager of chicken restaurant Nando's South Africa, which he joined in 2006. Nando's had always been known for its satirical tongue-in-cheek advertising, but with Chauke in the mix, the brand pushed the envelope even further through its commentary on current events and by saying what everyone was thinking.

Their 2009 'Change' campaign which poked fun at politician Julius Malema, then president of the African National Congress Youth League (ANCYL), was one of Chauke's most memorable. A puppet resembling Malema told South Africans that if they wanted *change* in the upcoming elections, they had to look no further than Nando's. Ordering a quarter peri-peri chicken with chips and a cool drink for R33.95 and paying with a R100 note, would get them R66.05 *change*, which is more than they'd paid for the meal.

The ANCYL threatened Nando's with militant action and demanded that the TV advertisement be withdrawn. "It was heated and controversial and led to me being summoned to the

ANC headquarters to account to its leadership. I was incredibly nervous," Chauke, now 37, recalls.

He left Nando's in 2010 – not because of his run-in with the ANCYL – to join MTV Networks Africa as director of marketing and communications, what many would consider a dream job. Chauke, a self-confessed Madonna-fanatic, says his most unforgettable moment at MTV was working at the MTV Europe Music Awards as part of the global communications team. "Meeting famous stars came with the job at MTV," he says.

But in 2012, after about two years at MTV, Chauke traded his cushy life and respectable salary for the unpredictable world of entrepreneurship by starting the Johannesburg-based advertising and communications agency DNA Brand Architects.

Although he never saw himself as an entrepreneur and always found the idea of "running your own business quite daunting", he did realise that he has been thinking like an entrepreneur at Nando's and MTV. "My approach to business was always entrepreneurial," says Chauke. "It's about trying to reach a goal and utilising all the tools you have at your disposal to reach that goal. It's as simple as that." He had also learnt that being innovative in an established global business often was much more complicated than doing something independently.

Launching DNA was, however, not a rash decision. From starting to think about it and registering the company to finally taking the plunge, took him six years. "I didn't think I was ready for it," he says. "I didn't think I had learnt enough."

During those six years in the corporate environment, Chauke had time to "stress test" his ideas and decide what would set his business apart and, by the time that he resigned, his vision was much clearer.

EARLY DAYS

When Chauke founded DNA, he was it – it was a one-man band. Although he had discussed his plan with possible business partners, nothing came of it. He was frustrated because, while they could have been "great partners", they didn't get his vision. "It was important to me that what I wanted to create was well understood."

Furthermore, he wanted to first figure things out and let the company grow organically until it was financially viable to bring partners or high-salaried employees on board. He didn't want others to take risks on his behalf.

There were no investors or bank loans either. DNA was founded with his personal savings alone. To this day, Chauke is proud that the company has never had an overdraft facility. "I feel more liberated when I don't owe too many people too much. I sleep better too."

All the same, he did make sure to line up a few consulting gigs so that there would be some money coming in. "I have capacity for risk but it's not very big. I want to feel that I have things under control. It was important to me to at least have some work to do. You can imagine what it's like going from an MTV salary to zero income."

Those early days were "difficult times". "I remember walking into a potential client's boardroom for a pitch and they asked, 'So, who are you and where are you from?' I said, 'I'm Sylvester from DNA Brand Architects.' To which they asked, 'Who is DNA Brand Architects? Which brands have you worked on?' Of course, the company hadn't worked on any. It humbled me.

"To tell the truth, I became depressed. It was very, very lonely, but the vision and my excitement about the company's potential kept me going."

Thanks to the reputation he had established at Nando's and MTV, work gradually began coming in. A few months in, he was able to employ an assistant and some months later another staff member. "Since then it's been building slowly but surely," he says.

DNA's first client was pay-TV operator Multichoice which signed them for the launch of *Keeping Up with the Kardashians*. It didn't bring in much money but it did help to build a portfolio of work for DNA as an agency without having to ride on Chauke's previous experience.

Another early client was Nedbank. Again, although the assignment wasn't very profitable, it was "really great, because Nedbank was a brand doing work that is visible". Working with Nedbank and Multichoice allowed DNA to show "that we've got the goods and we can deliver at that level".

He stresses the importance of getting a few jobs under your belt as soon as possible after starting out: "In the beginning it's not so much about the money but to establish a network and some credentials."

With time, DNA added a string of large clients to its portfolio. Among the highlights were the launch of South African Breweries' flavoured beer brand Flying Fish as well as Alfa Romeo's Stelvio SUV and handling mobile operator Vodacom's public relations and reputation management.

Thanks to the good relationship Chauke maintained with his previous employer, even after leaving the company, DNA was appointed to undertake the marketing and brand communication for the MTV Africa Music Awards. Chauke was upfront with the vice president of MTV about his plans before resigning and his response was that Chauke should let him know if he needed anything. "I said: 'Of course. I need business from you!'" To this day, he believes in the importance of never burning your bridges.

FROM A ONE-MAN BAND TO MANAGING A TEAM

Start-ups built on the skills of the founder often struggle to maintain the same quality output once the company begins to grow, and with more than 35 staff members, Chauke admits that maintaining standards is one of the most challenging aspects of his job. "If we lose what makes us unique in the market, we will be just like any other company."

That said, DNA has reached the stage where the team can deliver without necessarily involving Chauke every step of the way. "Getting too involved in the small things is not the best way to use my time," he explains. "A business must be able to run without having to depend on the CEO or founder. Right now, I don't know half the things that are happening in the company. That's very, very important. In fact, it makes me feel – for the first time in six years – that I actually have a business. Until now, I was merely building one."

When a piece of work is not up to scratch, he prefers inspiring the team to think bigger instead of becoming involved himself. "When I do get involved, it is to add value to the idea; to make it big, better, more exciting. It's not to interfere and do the work," he explains. Once the team is going again, he steps back and withdraws.

On a one-on-one level, Chauke also steers employees when

necessary. If someone is not performing as required, he invites them to his office for a calm, open conversation in the lounge. After starting by conveying his disappointment, Chauke usually suggests how and where they could improve. Only if he feels he is not getting through, will he act more assertively to make sure that his message "lands".

Developing his staff is important to him but he has had to learn that sometimes you have to let someone go when, even after counsel and support, the person is not progressing as fast as they should. "As young leaders we are generally scared to make these decisions, but we should."

Although the DNA environment is "open, easy, fun and cool", Chauke takes care to prevent it from becoming "too cool and too much fun" when it's necessary to knuckle down and get on with a project. In addition to keeping a paternal eye on things, Chauke concentrates on landing new clients and keeping DNA on track with his long-term vision. Their Cape Town office is about to open and he is investigating partnership opportunities in Nigeria. An alliance with a company in New York is also on the cards.

A typical day for Chauke goes as follows:

"Arrive at the office, get an understanding of what is needed from me
Attend a few strategic meetings and catch-ups
Follow-up calls where needed
Review of topline strategic work
Dream a little and put it down on paper
Client meetings where needed
Concept time
Negotiations and more negotiations

Take a walk around the office
Listen to music
Track performance across business KPIs
An occasional office dance or two!" (If he wasn't in advertising, Chauke says he would be a dancer.)

ROLLING WITH THE PUNCHES

As the company got bigger and making revenue targets and meeting payroll became real priorities, the business became much more demanding, says Chauke, who admits he is constantly stressed. "I had assumed that the start-up phase would be the toughest but it gets tougher as the business grows. Now that we are in our sixth year, it is much more challenging than before. With hindsight, the early days were a breeze."

One of his worst days was when DNA lost a major client. It was a company they had worked with for four years. When it underwent leadership changes, key members of the marketing team left and some departments merged. Although they were pleased with DNA's work, the new management required a different type of agency. So Chauke received a letter to terminate their relationship. Financially, it was a big blow. "It was a client that paid well and quickly. In other words, the best kind of client." Luckily DNA didn't have to lay off staff, but still had to move quickly to plug the hole. It made Chauke realise that "you're never safe in business".

"As an entrepreneur, no two months or years are ever the same. You get great years; you get bad years. You get amazing quarters and bad quarters," he notes.

Internally, he has been thrown a few curve balls too. When a member of his leadership team acted in an incongruous manner towards staff members, the situation threatened to compromise the entire company. Addressing the matter and acting decisively was a big learning experience for Chauke. The person eventually left the company but took many of DNA's ideas with him and tried to poach their clients and staff.

While the world's biggest and most respected companies also go through incidents like this, younger business owners are often not prepared for it and Chauke cautions, "You will have to deal with bad relationships, bad breakups and partnerships that don't work out." As a manager, he says, you should get comfortable with the fact that "not everybody in the business has its best interests at heart".

Chauke's mentor, Nando's co-founder Robbie Brozin, helped him to steer through such difficult times and moments of doubt and confusion. "He has helped me to deal with dishonesty and betrayal, lack of self-belief, scaling the company and how to remain a good man in a shrewd and often unforgiving business environment."

HELPING AFRICAN BRANDS SCALE GLOBALLY

Before Nando's, Chauke had worked at advertising agencies such as Ogilvy & Mather and FCB Africa. He says over the past decade there has been a huge shift in the marketing and communications industry, with client budgets under pressure and greater competition. "It's definitely tougher today to be in this business. It's volatile and it's unpredictable." Back in the day the industry was dominated by a handful of large agencies, but "nowadays there are a plethora of players. Many, many small players that are also eating at the pie."

It no longer is just a matter of running a TV advertisement or placing an ad in a newspaper. Technology is forcing companies to think "broader and more holistically". "Consumers are not bystanders to marketing messages anymore. Beyond seeing your ad, they can question it and engage with it on social media with lightning speed. It means that we, as marketing professionals, have to think across all the platforms customers engage on. Not any more is it a case of sending a one-way message. Customers are interacting with brands and brands have to be prepared for it," he explains.

Chauke's dream client is Apple: "I love a bold brand with strong leadership, powerful vision and style." He is even more passionate about playing a part in building "African brands that vibrate on high streets around the world".

Chauke believes that companies on the continent don't deliberately plan to build global brands and mentions that the 2018 Brand Finance Global 500 list of the world's 500 most valuable brands doesn't include one name from Africa. "Africa is great at building businesses but not good at building brands," he says, and points to Nando's as one of the few African brands that have managed to scale globally.

"I would like to play a part in making businesses on the continent aware of the need for brand building, the need for scale and the need for world domination instead of concentrating on local markets only. I'd love to be part of writing that story."

14.

Yoadan Tilahun

Showing Ethiopia how to throw an event

By Jaco Maritz & Jeanette Clark

Yoadan Tilahun left the city of her birth, Addis Ababa, in 1993 to attend college in the United States. She went with the intention of returning after four years but ended up staying for 15 years.

"Even though it was great in the United States, I always felt like a visitor. I worked there, met my husband, who is also Ethiopian, and we had two of our kids there but it never felt like home. There was always something missing," she says.

The 42-year-old founder and CEO of Flawless Events, an event management agency based in Addis Ababa, remembers the day she knew her future lay in her home country like yesterday. "In 2007, I took a couple of months off and came to Addis with our children. Within two weeks I knew this is the feeling I was looking for," she remembers. "After 15 years in the States it took only two weeks in Addis to feel like I had finally come home."

She admits that her return came at the exact right time for her entrepreneurial spirit and venture to flourish. The Ethiopia she grew up in, the one ruled by a communist regime from 1974 to 1987, was a thing of the past.

"I always tell people that the beauty of doing business in Ethiopia is that whatever you do, it is such a virgin market that you will stand out if you do it well," she says. Flawless Events began by doing one or two events a year. Now Yoadan and her all-woman team run over 50 events annually.

LIVING AWAY FROM HOME: THE ORIGINS OF FLAWLESS

Yoadan was born and raised in Addis Ababa as the only girl in her parents' house alongside her two brothers. She was the only one to attend the Lycée Guébré-Mariam, a French international school which was established in 1947, for no particular reason except that her "mother liked women who spoke French". "It was rather difficult to figure out why I was speaking a language no one else in my family spoke," she laughs. The Lycée provided her with connections which would last a lifetime and some of the friends she made there became her co-founders when she launched Flawless Events years later in the greater Washington metropolitan area in the United States.

Like her, her brothers were sent abroad for their tertiary studies, her older brother went to the United Kingdom while her younger brother also went to the States.

"I was 17 when I went. This was pre-Google times and just figuring out where I was going to go to college was a challenge. I ended up in Nebraska and then moved to Missouri where I did my first degree in international business. After four years I was done. The economic situation in Ethiopia was changing, and I wanted to come home, but my parents said I had to get a second degree before I returned."

Yoadan completed an MBA in international business in Memphis, again with the aim of going home immediately afterwards. Again her parents asked her to stay on, this time to gain work experience. And so four years in the States became 15.

She eventually moved to Washington, progressing to a job with the World Bank, and married Mirafe Marcos. By then, she and three old friends had already started a business on the side that arranged social and corporate events under the name Flawless.

"We had been living the good life, partying and working, having no specific purpose to speak of," Yoadan says of the period leading up to the establishment of Flawless in 2004. "Month to month we were running out of money and started asking ourselves what we could do to supplement our regular incomes. We were attending events by African institutions and always felt that they were a bit messy. That is how we got the idea to start an events company," she says. The name was born during a brainstorming session where the emphasis kept coming back to running seamless, perfect – flawless – events.

After organising a few events, two of the four partners realised that the industry was not for them, but Yoadan was hooked. "I loved the rush of it, the stress, that feeling when everything comes together. It felt awesome!"

Three years later, her small events company had made a name for itself in the circles in which Yoadan and Mirafe were living and working. Their second son had just been born and they were once again discussing the possibility of moving back to Ethiopia.

Mirafe encouraged Yoadan to take some time off and to visit her home country for the first time since she left in 1992. It was the only way to see if it was a country where she could envision them building a future for themselves and their children.

While in Addis Ababa, a friend who had just returned home

from the States to practise medicine asked her to extend her stay and help him to host a medical conference. Mirafe immediately encouraged her to give it a go and she rented shared office space with another acquaintance, registered her business and pulled off an extremely successful event for more than 500 delegates in April 2008. Flawless in Ethiopia was officially born.

STARTING FROM SCRATCH ON ANOTHER CONTINENT

Yoadan says she always had a fall-back plan at the back of her mind during those early days. If the events gig didn't work out, she believed that she would find employment in Addis Ababa quite easily with her qualifications. When she now talks about the success she has achieved, it is often with a pinch of self-deprecating disbelief that it actually happened. She credits her husband as her "thought partner" throughout her personal and professional journey. Often, when she didn't believe in herself, he encouraged her to take the bull by the horns.

"There was one other events company in Addis, a very large one, and most people said I would not be able to compete with them. That was a strange concept to me, as I didn't really want to compete with them. I believed the market was bigger than what they were doing. I took it one event at a time and growth came gradually," she says.

Yoadan loved the learning curve as well as educating businesses in Addis Ababa about the benefits of having an events company. At the time, larger corporates believed they didn't need more than an office assistant or secretary to put their events together. "After attending a few events Flawless had hosted, they began to understand why having an events organiser is an advantage."

That very first medical conference was challenging. She did not yet have a trusted vendor network and things such as advertising and registration still had to be done manually and in person. Yoadan drove around the city to put up posters with her personal mobile number on them. Because the medical fraternity in the country were hungry for continuous education opportunities and attendance was free for local doctors, she was bombarded with calls from prospective attendees.

"We had dial-up internet," Yoadan says and laughs when she remembers the awful dial-up sound every time she went online to make arrangements for the conference. In hindsight, she lists connectivity as one of the biggest challenges in those early years.

Word-of-mouth testimonials and references from the first conference led to the second event, another medical conference, where Flawless Events, in other words, Yoadan, achieved another success. Next came a small workshop for a cement company. For all of them, she leveraged her network and community of friends in Addis Ababa, which she believes contributed to her initial growth.

"We were a community of Ethiopians who had returned after working and studying abroad who wanted one another to succeed. We were like-minded and supported one another," she remembers.

GROWTH IN ETHIOPIA AND BEYOND

The event that was the catalyst for substantial growth and cemented Flawless' reputation for innovation and creativity came in 2010. Fred Swaniker, the co-founder of the African Leadership Academy, wanted to start a movement of African business leaders as an extension of the academy: he called it the African Leadership Network (ALN). As Addis Ababa is the seat of the African Union, he had the vision to host the inaugural summit in the city. A mutual friend introduced Swaniker to Yoadan.

"Since it was just myself and the one other events company in the city, he met with me and the competitor, but said he liked my energy better," Yoadan says of winning the contract. Then came the innovative, out-of-the-box ideas from Swaniker, something that definitely set the final event apart, but which also challenged Yoadan to up her game and rise to the challenge.

"Fred came up with the wildest ideas and called in the middle of the night when a thought hit him. He wanted the original African Union hall to be opened so that the invited delegates could sit where their country leaders sat. He wanted a debate with the Ethiopian Prime Minister on how young business leaders could have a part in political decision-making and the future of the continent," she recites the items on the list given to her. The Somali-Canadian musician K'naan's song *Wavin' Flag* was popular that year because of its association with the football world cup in South Africa and Swaniker wanted Ethiopian dancers to perform to it at the conference. He also wanted a TED-style auditorium, which Addis Ababa did not have.

"After all of this input I was freaking out but said, 'Sure, no problem Fred. We can do it'," Yoadan laughs. Her biggest challenge was to convince the Sheraton hotel to change its main ballroom into an amphitheatre-style set-up in the format of TED conferences, only to be told by Swaniker, once the Sheraton had transformed the hall to her specifications, that it was no longer necessary.

"At the end of the day, everything came together. The room

was full of the who's who of Africa living and working all over the world. The energy was great. They were all blown away by one another. To this day I don't think we have done anything as impactful – not in terms of production nor the level of speakers or the quality of attendees who had gathered in one room to talk about transformative ideas for Africa. We had to deliver to a very high level and we did – while making sure that everything was authentically African," she says. The event gave Flawless credibility and soon offers to arrange other events started coming in.

"That event put us on the map. We were getting calls non-stop from people who wanted events that were on the same level," Yoadan remembers. It was also the year in which she appointed her first employee, an office assistant to help keep track of the books, bumping up the team to two.

The other event which stood out for her, purely because of its magnitude and scale, took place a year after the ALN launch. The Ethiopian government had won the bid to host ICASA 2011, the annual International Conference on AIDS and Sexually Transmitted Infections in Africa, and Flawless was selected as the local partner of the international agency running the event.

"It was a big deal for the country. We had to find between 7 000 and 10 000 beds in the city. We were calling and driving around to find every single available hotel bed in Addis. It was an eye opener in terms of what we had available in the city. It was a learning process on how to work with government. It made me humble and taught me patience. Also, it taught me to juggle 10 million things at once," she says. The same year she hired another strong employee to assist with running parallel events. The team had begun to grow.

Now Flawless has events in several countries on the continent in their portfolio, including the African Philanthropy Forum in Kigali, Rwanda; an African Venture Capital Association workshop in Dar es Salaam, Tanzania; and various event elements for the ICT advisory and networking organisation Extensia in Burkina Faso, Tanzania, Mauritius, Zimbabwe and Nigeria.

Despite being called Flawless, there has been disappointments and failures. Yoadan does not like remembering them but she did learn from these experiences and they spurred her on to plan even more fiercely to prevent them from happening again.

"To this day I have nightmares about an event we organised for a German client. Everything was going perfectly. I had two or three people working with me at the time and the client was comfortable with my team and me." Yoadan chose a particular sound equipment supplier over another to save the client money. But on the day, during the opening session, the equipment failed. The interpreters couldn't do their job due to the feedback in their earphones and the audience could not hear the speakers. She was devastated.

"I still wish that the floor had opened up and swallowed me. You could see the disappointment and frustration on the client's face. After that, everything went to pieces. We had lost the client's trust. Everyone in the client's team started doubting us and what we were saying, even decisions that had already been finalised. I lost sleep over it for the next few months," she recalls. "Just the thought of it still embarrasses me."

LESSONS IN INTEGRITY AND QUALITY

When asked about the smartest decision she has made to grow her business, she answers without hesitation: keeping the quality of their work exceptionally high and always doing business with integrity and honesty.

If she could do it all again, she would hire capable, smart people earlier on as it would have helped to grow the business in a more structured way. "We are 10 years down the road and I am only now realising that the company is worthy of smart people. It is no longer a tiny company or my small little passion – it has outgrown me," she says. At the same time she admits that part of it was just her mentality and controlling personality. She struggled to let go and trust others to do the work. "I am less forgiving of mistakes than the clients."

If young people romanticise entrepreneurship, she says it can be ascribed to entrepreneurs' unwillingness to be open about their struggles and the hurdles of working on the continent. "If we talked about it more openly, it would make a difference. Not everyone can be an entrepreneur. Some people need to be career-oriented hard workers to allow businesses to succeed and thrive. We should talk about professionalism and the discipline of work in all aspects and not only when it comes to entrepreneurs," she says.

She believes the oft-heard entrepreneurial advice that you have to have passion for your industry. "If you are passionate about what you are doing, you will be able to weather the strongest storms," she says. Her advice to entrepreneurs in Africa is simple and concise: "Honesty pays off. Having integrity pays off.

"I was lucky to come to Ethiopia when I did. The industry is a lot more competitive now. I was lucky that I never had to worry about where I would sleep if things fell apart. I was lucky to have a really positive community supporting me at the start.

I would say about 50 per cent of the success I have achieved was luck," Yoadan states.

"The rest was super hard work and discipline."

15.

Mossadeck Bally
West African hotel group built on an appetite for risk

By Jeanette Clark

For the first nine years of his life – while he was growing up in Niamey, the capital of Niger, on the banks of the Niger river – it looked like Mossadeck Bally was set to follow in his father and grandfather's footsteps and enter the world of trading. A born businessman, Bally's father left his home country of Mali when the then strict socialist regime under President Modibo Keïta forbade private economic activity, to make a home for himself and his family in their neighbouring country. There, the life of a commodities trader was ingrained in the young Bally and his father continued to import and export goods when the family moved back to Mali in 1970, two years after the 1968 coup d'état that resulted in a somewhat liberalised economy.

Bally's grandfather originally sold salt bars from the salt mines in Mali's Taoudenni region approximately 650km north of the ancient city of Timbuktu. His father initially followed suit and transported the salt first by camel and then, from Timbuktu, on small boats which travelled into the heart of the country. Just before the move to Niamey, he started trading fabric imported from Europe. At the beginning of the 1980s the business evolved again into the trading of rice, sugar, wheat flour, tea, tomato paste and other products sourced internationally and sold locally in shops.

"Whenever we had a vacation from school, we spent it in my father's shops. I believe this developed in me, at a very early stage, a love for entrepreneurship. I was fascinated by my father – always travelling, hosting business dinners at home, welcoming people from all around the world," Bally, now 57, remembers.

Despite having a grandfather who was a "famous trader from Timbuktu" and a father who was "one of the biggest traders in West Africa", Bally eventually chose an entirely different route. He is well known and internationally respected for founding the Azalaï Hotels group and building it into a thriving company, which has earned him accolades such as the 2011 African Development Bank's African Business Leadership Award.

The group's name is his tribute to his family roots. "Azalaï" (pronounced as-ah-lie) is the Tuareg Berber name for the route followed by camel caravans twice a year to transport salt from the north of Mali to Timbuktu.

LAYING THE FOUNDATIONS

Azalaï Hotels has 10 properties in six African countries (Mali, Burkina Faso, Guinea Bissau, Benin, Mauritania and Côte d'Ivoire) with four projects underway in Senegal, Niger, Guinea and Cameroon. It is also in negotiations regarding developments in Nigeria, Ghana, Liberia and Sierra Leone.

The group is valued at more than $110 million, has approximately 1 000 direct employees and provides indirect employment to roughly 2 000 people.

To get to this point, Bally started in the import-export business and worked alongside his father after completing a bac-calauréat (a French post-high school qualification required to gain university entry) in Marseille, France, and obtaining a bachelor's degree in business administration with a major in finance at the University of San Francisco in the United States.

"I always thought I would spend my whole career doing what my father did. After 10 years, though, I wanted to go into industry, to diversify. I had the feeling that it would allow me to be more impactful on the economy of my country and to create more value and more jobs."

His first idea was to start a mango factory to capitalise on Mali's production capacity for this tropical stone fruit. The factory would process the fruit into juice and cordials for sale to major international beverage companies. Bally was well on his way and had already finalised the business plan and concluded a trip to Europe to investigate machinery suppliers, when one of his trading partners, while on a visit to Bamako, suggested the hospitality industry.

"Suppliers often came to see me and always complained about the quality of the city's hotels – all of them were state-owned and state-run," Bally says. Once he determined that the hospitality industry creates many jobs, allows for value to be added and brings foreign exchange into the country, Bally jumped at the idea.

The timing was perfect. In 1994, the Malian government put out a tender to sell a hotel in Bamako in a move towards privatisation. Thanks to the contacts Bally had built up through the family business, he was able to get an expert consultant to help him with the bid – which he won.

A loan of $1 million from the Bank of Africa Mali allowed him to buy the hotel from the government and a loan of a further $1 million from the International Finance Corporation (IFC), a subsidiary of the World Bank, enabled him to refurbish it. Suddenly Bally was the owner of the Grand Hotel Bamako, the oldest hotel in Mali's capital, that was built in 1952 under French colonial rule. It was to become the first hotel in Bally's Azalaï Hotels group.

The initial months after reopening in 1995 were difficult. Bally ascribes it to a period without much business, as the hotel first had to gain clientele, and experienced big cash flow problems. Within a year, though, it was profitable.

Although it was a tough period, it was, in some ways, good old times. "The days of turning a profit within a year are no more. Then, we were operating in a unique niche environment where no other hotels were run to international standards. Now competition is fierce and there are international hotel chains in almost every location we are in." Azalaï's competition now includes big names like Radisson and Sheraton.

Bally's hotel business grew quickly, first as a chain of independent hotels before being grouped as Azalaï Hotels, as he began to capitalise on other West African governments which moved to privatise hotel properties during the early years of the century. After purchasing land for a second hotel in Bamako, which opened in January 2000, a privatisation bid for a government-owned hotel in Burkina Faso was finalised in 2004. This was followed by two others from the governments of Guinea Bissau and Benin in 2007 and 2008 respectively.

"After this there were no more state-owned hotel bids for a while and we started looking at greenfield projects, which naturally takes a lot more time to finalise – usually around four years. The only other privatisation opportunity that materialised was the hotel in Mauritania in 2016," he says.

GREAT RISKS BRING GREAT REWARDS

Almost without exception, Azalaï's hotels are situated in countries categorised as either post-conflict or conflict-afflicted
nations.

This brings a unique set of challenges but Bally considers
them simply as risks that have to be identified, tackled and mit-
igated; just like any other risk facing young and growing businesses.

When he and his team moved to establish a presence in
Abidjan in Côte d'Ivoire in 2016, many of the investors who
had supported Azalaï over the years felt that the group was
not yet ready to invest and compete in a more developed market. "With the operation that we have in Abidjan today, we feel
we were right in moving from exclusively frontier markets and
into bigger economies. Our risk is well spread," he says.

With a large part of his business in countries prone to political unrest and instability, Bally has had to make the decision a
couple of times to close a hotel when a coup d'état was underway or had just taken place. During the 2012 coup and conflict
in Mali, he was forced to close two hotels in the country for
eight months. Luckily, the group's size allowed them to retain
their employees. "We have since taken out political risk cover
with insurance companies. We didn't have it before, but we are
now covered by a company that reinsures with Lloyd's of London," he says. "But with high risk, you also have high returns.

"That is our job as entrepreneurs, to take risks. I would say
my strongest point was being born and raised in an entrepreneurial family where I developed the sense of taking risks very
early on. I got a good education but have an even better family
education, thanks to my parents. I always tell my kids that I got

my real MBA on the ground while working with my father, not at school."

Having learnt the value of hard work and integrity as a child, he now imparts it to young entrepreneurs. "I tell them to always get advice from a mentor and to know that nothing which is beautiful can be achieved quickly."

Like all entrepreneurs, the first hurdle Bally had to overcome was to find the money to buy and refurbish the Grand Hotel and he says, "For someone who really wants to start a business, financing is often the biggest challenge, especially if it's a start-up."

Bally's contacts from the family business certainly helped in this regard. The IFC officer who assisted him to find a consultant to help with the bid for the Grand Hotel was someone he had met while working with his father. It is a connection which has lasted for more than 20 years and Bally and the IFC still have a working relationship.

The second hurdle was finding qualified contractors to refurbish the hotel on a limited budget and hotel staff who could provide superior service. With the help of the African Management Services Company (AMSCO), Bally found a hotel manager, Bertrand Boyer. AMSCO is an IFC/ United Nations project that helps African small and medium-sized enterprises to find high-level managers and subsidises their salaries. "I would not have been able to bring in a high-level expatriate and seasoned hotelier like Boyer otherwise," says Bally.

"Human resources remain my biggest problem. The countries Azalaï are in haven't invested in training in the hospitality industry. I was fortunate to have a French national as the manager of the first hotel who could train our Malian and other African employees."

Azalaï Hotels now has its own hospitality training academy in Bamako that provides one year's vocational training to students wanting to go into hotels, restaurants and diplomatic households.

A further challenge was "how to balance a very busy, time-consuming professional life with having a personal life". "At some point, you will have to compromise. The price I had to pay was quite high – my first wife and I had a divorce. We have three beautiful and successful boys."

Now that Azalaï has grown and has a large staff contingent, he does enjoy a more balanced life but is not sure whether it is because he has finally learnt how to strike a balance or because he is not as involved in the day-to-day operations. "I am married for the second time and can say that I am a very fulfilled person. It is easier for an established entrepreneur to find this balance than for a start-up," he says.

WHY NOT SIT BACK AND ENJOY HIS SUCCESS?

"When people ask what motivates me because I have nothing left to prove, I always have the same answer: I want to create more jobs and have a greater impact on a country's economy. It is not financial satisfaction that I am looking for. I had that as a trader." He says passionately, "It fuels me on further when I see the women who sell products to our hotels, the butcheries who provide the meat, the taxes we pay to local governments, all the young people who find employment and don't have to leave for Europe or work as slaves in Libya or have to die on a small boat in the Mediterranean Sea."

His greatest fear is not being able to pass on his company to someone who will keep developing it, whether it is to his children or an outside buyer. "I really want Azalaï Hotels to remain an African brand and to continue growing. I fear that if my children do not want to take over, I will have to sell it to an international company that will take down the brand and manage it as a subsidiary."

Despite business challenges such as keeping a hotel open in conflict-torn countries, his enthusiasm for Africa remains undiminished: "I am quite confident that the continent will develop. I am confident about the future of Africa and its economies as more and more African entrepreneurs are coming to the fore and developing more champions. There is tremendous opportunity."

While intra-African investment is climbing, Bally acknowledges the continent still has to sell itself to attract foreign direct investment to be able to achieve its potential. For him, it is a matter of disseminating information, advertising and communicating better. "Perhaps bigger African media houses should talk about the positives in Africa instead of having only international media talking about what is not going well. There is a very high risk perception of the continent. Some of it is real, of course, but most of it is not."

A few years ago, news reports indicated that there was a plan in the offing at Azalaï Hotels about listing on a stock exchange. Bally says this has not changed but it has been postponed. "Today we don't have problems accessing finance. Thus, strategically, we think we can push the listing out two to three more years," he explains.

"When speaking to businesspeople who are new to Africa, I always tell them that they must have a long-term plan. Africa is not a continent where you can take a short-term view. I learnt this from working next to my late father. He was very patient and never became discouraged," Bally says. "You have to be optimistic and resilient to succeed in Africa."

16.

Jennifer Bash

Adding value to everyday staples

By Oluwabusayomi Sotunde & Jaco Maritz

Tanzanian businesswoman Jennifer Bash says entrepreneurs typically approach a new business in two ways. The first is to focus on providing a solution to a problem, while the second is to choose an industry based purely on its profit potential. "If you provide a solution to a problem, the money will come anyway. But if money is your starting point and the company doesn't make as much as you had anticipated, you will be out of business very soon because you have nothing else that motivates you," she says.

The problem she solved through Alaska Tanzania Industries was a shortage of properly packaged and branded local food products. "Tanzania, like most African countries, is blessed with an abundance of natural resources, but not enough businesses are focusing on the processing and packaging of those resources into consumer goods," says Bash.

"We had eggs that were imported from the Gulf and the United Kingdom in supermarkets, not because we did not have eggs in Tanzania, but because the eggs we had were not branded and packaged to supermarket standards and therefore did not make it onto the shelves. It made me realise that the problem is not production because there are lots of well-processed foods. Most producers fail when it comes to packaging and branding. Product packaging plays an increasingly important role in consumers' buying decisions."

The company's team of 25 employees processes, packages and distributes a range of food products, including eggs, rice, maize flour and sunflower oil. Alaska Tanzania has become a reputable name in Tanzania and, in 2016, it was recognised as one of the top 50 local brands by the Tanzania Private Sector Foundation and the Tanzania Bureau of Standards. The following year, Bash was named East Africa Young Business Leader of the Year at the 2017 All Africa Business Leaders Awards.

She grew her business from humble beginnings, starting out with a small broiler chicken venture in Dar es Salaam, which produced fresh chicken meat. However, she says, "The supermarkets and hotels we targeted wanted frozen chicken, not fresh. Due to the unreliable power supply, we didn't have refrigerated rooms to handle the supply."

So, they turned to layer chickens, as eggs don't require such a comprehensive cold chain. The change in strategy worked and soon they were supplying eggs to several supermarkets.

Then, in 2008, Bash left for the United States to further her studies and entrusted the business to a capable manager – or so she thought. During her time away, the manager steered the company towards financial ruin. One of the reasons was that he had raised his own chickens on the side and bought feed for his birds on credit through the company, which saddled the business with significant debt.

"Also, he was not supplying the clients we used to supply. He couldn't keep those clients and ended up supplying the informal markets, selling eggs on a very small scale. We were not making money," explains Bash.

In 2011, the business received an investment from a family friend who owned fishing businesses in Alaska and was on a visit to look for expansion opportunities in Tanzania. He liked the idea of her chicken farm and provided funding. He later returned to the States and his contribution lives on in the company name, Alaska Tanzania.

TRANSFORMING THE BUSINESS

When she returned to Tanzania in 2012, Bash was dismayed by the state of the business. She fired the manager and changed the company's strategy to source eggs only from smallholder farmers. "We realised many farmers were doing a great job raising chickens but that they were not good at marketing the products they were producing," says Bash.

Through attractive packaging and branding, she differentiated Alaska Tanzania's eggs from its competitors'. Quality is also key to the company's value proposition. For instance, she knows her customers are particular about the colour of the yolk. "Most customers prefer yellow yolk eggs. Inconsistency of the chicken feed formula may result in the yolk being too orange or white," explains Bash.

The appearance and taste of the eggs are largely influenced by the type of chicken feed a farmer uses, which is why Alaska Tanzania carefully chooses the farmers it works with. "To join our network, we ask farmers to fill in a registration form and we profile them thoroughly. We source farmers' produce in batches and sell in batches to ensure quality control. Our aim is to sell products that can be traced to their origins," she says.

Starting with a team of only two staff back in 2013, Bash

gradually hired more employees and handed over control of certain aspects of the business to others. "Running a company with a team of two staff members means wearing many hats. I was the one handling the core work of the business, as well as other tasks like marketing, accounting, human resources and distribution. I delivered products with my own car. Delegating tasks is crucial when growth is the goal: it frees you from micromanagement and allows you to work on the business rather than in the business."

As Alaska Tanzania landed more supermarket clients and increased its distribution capacity, it became viable to introduce more products to its range. Its first new product was rice from the Mbeya region in the southwest of the country, which the company bought from farmers and packaged and branded under Alaska Tanzania. "We approached all the supermarkets that sold our eggs, to also carry our rice brand."

Then came maize flour. "If a Tanzanian hasn't had *ugali* (a starchy dish made from maize flour) today, they will tomorrow," she said in an earlier interview. "For many Tanzanians, the routine is *ugali* for lunch and rice for dinner. So, not a day goes by without someone consuming it." Another product is sunflower oil, which the company sources, packages, brands and distributes.

While diversifying a product portfolio opens new revenue streams, Bash cautions against introducing new items before the current ones are well established. "You don't want to concentrate on new products and then end up losing focus on the existing product lines or spreading your resources too thin."

Alaska Tanzania's expansion has not been without hurdles. One expensive mistake was in 2016 when Bash bought a maize milling plant without doing enough research. After she had taken out a bank loan and bought the machinery, Bash discovered that the land on which they wanted to build the factory did not have access to electricity and providing their own power would have been too costly. The machinery was sitting idle, while the bank loan had to be repaid from the first month. It took her a year to find the rented premises from which Alaska Tanzania currently processes its maize.

Sourcing directly from farmers also comes with its challenges, particularly when dealing with individual smallholders. Alaska Tanzania has therefore opted to work with groups of farmers and partnered with other stakeholders in the agricultural value chain, such as development agencies and NGOs, to mitigate risks.

She is proud of Alaska Tanzania's role in developing the country's agricultural sector. "We are empowering rural smallholder farmers by providing them with access to input supplies and training on good agricultural practices. In return, this allows us to source quality outputs."

Having a sure buyer for their crops also enables farmers to get bank loans to purchase inputs and equipment, which further boosts their productivity. "From the financial institutions' viewpoint, farmers are risky business. If farmers have a guaranteed market like Alaska Tanzania, the banks can lend them money because they are sure of the repayments," says Bash.

In addition, Alaska Tanzania is also developing a digital platform, called Agrisoko, which will provide farmers with information on commodity prices, the availability of buyers and sellers, and guidance on best practices in harvesting and disease management.

STANDING OUT IN A CROWDED MARKET

Alaska Tanzania sells mostly to large supermarkets, which include a combination of international retailers – such as Food Lover's Market and Game – and locally owned grocers. Finding shelf space in these stores has become much easier over the years. "Previously, we had to chase after every supermarket and offer discounts to get shelf space. Now, when a new shop opens, they email us to request to do business with us," says Bash.

The supermarkets' strict payment terms – typically 30 to 45 days – mean that suppliers must have sufficient working capital. "The more supermarkets you supply, the less liquid you are. You must have enough cash to be able to keep on supplying them between payments," notes Bash.

Whereas the company used to have only a handful of international rivals, a plethora of domestic players have now entered the market. "Back in the day it was us and three imported brands on the eggs shelf, but now supermarkets hardly import eggs at all. My competitors are all local brands."

Alaska Tanzania's competitive advantage is its quality control systems and the convenience of its products. "Customers demand quality from Alaska Tanzania. If you look at eggs, for instance, ours are a little pricier than our competitors' but they still move quickly," Bash points out. Pricing, she says, is not part of the company's market strategy. Rather, Alaska Tanzania's credibility lies in its "quality and traceability".

"Also, many of our competitors' products are only available in one or two supermarkets because they struggle with the 45-day payment terms," she says. Moreover, due to the seasonal nature of agriculture, many other producers don't supply throughout the year whereas Alaska Tanzania's products are on the shelves year-round. "We make sure we maintain our supply chain and that we don't lose our customers by giving them a reason to try another brand."

With little initial capital, Bash has built Alaska Tanzania into a respected player in the food industry. She says a lack of money shouldn't keep entrepreneurs from pursuing their ambitions. They should leverage all the resources at their disposal, including their skills and networks, and seek out partnerships to do the things they can't do alone.

However, 100 per cent commitment and a willingness to make sacrifices are essential. "For instance, you might want to go on holiday, but if your company can't support it, then you have to be willing to forgo that. Sometimes you might not even be able to pay yourself a salary," she says.

Once money starts coming in, it's important to reinvest it. "Rather than rewarding yourself, put it back into the company because the rewards that come later will be even greater.

"Do not despise small beginnings," she says. "Start where you are with what you have. Don't become the victim of analysis paralysis. Don't fear failures, but recognise them as learning opportunities and necessary stepping stones to success. Your ability to grow a small venture into a large company depends on your vision, drive, discipline and determination."

17.

Jesse Moore

Thinking out of the box to power over 600 000 homes with solar energy

By Sven Hugo

For the majority of people in developed countries, electricity is a given. You press a switch and a light comes on; squeeze a remote control button and the TV screen flickers; flip a lever on the kettle and water boils.

But for many in rural Africa, light is emitted from a kerosene lamp, heat from fire, and energy for a radio or torch from short-lived, expensive batteries. It's a reality that permeates every aspect of daily life in villages across the continent. More than 640 million people in Africa don't have access to reliable grid-connected electricity.

In 2012, M-KOPA Solar entered the Kenyan market with solar home systems and now is the torchbearer for off-the-grid electricity in Africa. Its entry-level product consists of an eight-watt solar panel, a lithium battery, four light bulbs, a rechargeable torch and a cable to charge mobile phones. The more advanced home system comes complete with a 24-inch flat screen TV with free-to-air channels and a radio.

Users rig the solar panel, about the size of a standard pillow, in the sunniest spot on their roof, hook it up to the supplied appliances and wait for the sun to do its thing – electricity from above.

Six years on, more than 600 000 homes in Kenya and Uganda are fitted with M-KOPA solar units and CEO and co-founder Jesse Moore believes the numbers will grow into the millions. M-KOPA has received numerous accolades, among them being included in MIT's 2017 list of the top 50 smartest businesses in the world, which puts it in the company of Amazon and SpaceX.

The introduction of solar energy has dramatically changed life for many people in rural communities. In Kenya, a woman explained to a journalist from *Msafiri* magazine that solar electricity has provided them with light that allows children to do their homework at night, and adults to work, which includes milking their cows. A solar-charged torch lights the path to the outhouse otherwise wrapped in complete darkness.

Key to M-KOPA's success is its innovative technology and affordable payment plan. Customers buy the entry-level kit for an initial deposit of approximately $30. Daily instalments to the equivalent of about 50 cents are then paid for a period of up to 420 days. Once payment has been completed, customers own the system outright. In Kenya, payments are made via mobile money platform M-Pesa, which has over 20 million subscribers. Sensors on the equipment allow M-KOPA to regulate usage based upon payments received – if a customer stops paying and runs out of credit, the system is shut down remotely and ceases to function.

INVENTING A NEW INDUSTRY

Canadian-born Jesse Moore studied at the University of North Carolina at Chapel Hill, during which he did a semester abroad at the University of Cape Town and "did a fair bit of travelling around sub-Saharan Africa". This sparked a curiosity in international development as a career. He worked for a large humanitarian charity for five years and became increasingly interested in small-scale business development and "doing business that would help the typical beneficiaries of charity". This led to an MBA at the Saïd Business School at Oxford University, after which he worked for M-Pesa as a consultant. "M-Pesa was an opportune business model and technology to get to know quickly, and from this starting point we came up with the idea for M-KOPA," he says. *Kopa* is the Swahili word for *borrow*.

Moore moved to Nairobi in 2010 to start the business. M-KOPA is technically not an energy company, but rather a consumer finance business that just happened to start out with financing solar energy systems.

With its solar system, M-KOPA wants to replace kerosene – which is expensive, unhealthy and unsafe – as an energy source. "I think kerosene lighting is a massive pain point. People don't like the fumes, they don't like the cost, they don't like the quality of light and they don't like the danger. There are millions and millions of homes that rely on kerosene every day," says Moore.

M-KOPA based the pricing of its solar systems on market research and focus groups. After establishing a good estimate of what people were spending on energy, such as kerosene, they priced their systems to be cheaper. "Neglected customers don't have a wide range of quality services and usually are open to a better offer," Moore explains. "This is typically a very large market."

The litmus test for any company, he believes, is its products and whether someone is willing to pay for it. "When M-KOPA reached its first thousand customers, I thought that maybe we found a thousand crazy people willing to buy what we sell. When we hit ten thousand, I realised there can't be that many crazy people out there. But there's just something about making the first sales and realising you have a product people are willing to pay for and seeing the potential of scaling it up."

Moore always wanted to create a profitable company at the expense of none, or with "no trade-off". "If you take a leapfrogging technology and focus on an underserved, neglected customer-base and provide them with a winning service, you can remain profitable and feel good about all aspects of the business." That the company does its part for the environment, he calls "the cherry on top". Not many industries can say the same. "When you apply business models to serve low-income consumers, there is a real opportunity to create a win-win scenario."

His office overlooks the M-KOPA call centre where 200 agents are constantly communicating with customers. "Having the call centre front and centre of the business – at the main campus – and the idea that the voice of the customer is being heard nearby, illustrates the message we've always given our customers," he says. "It's critical to our business model."

Partnerships, too, are crucial to the success of M-KOPA and its alliance with mobile network operator Safaricom, which owns the M-Pesa mobile money platform, is symbiotic. Through M-KOPA, Safaricom clients can charge their phones and thus make more phone calls. "We also save our customers money, and collect payments through M-Pesa," Moore explains. "These synergies are very helpful." M-KOPA must at first have seemed a great corporate social responsibility initiative, but Safaricom soon realised it was becoming a significant client in terms of the volume of business it was bringing in.

Today, many have followed the M-KOPA business model but the company continues to build on its first-mover advantage. "We were first and we worked extremely hard," says Moore. "You raise capital, you hire people and build systems, but you have to remain determined," he explains. "To build something on the scale of M-KOPA today would require a lot of determination."

M-KOPA has now expanded its offering to other merchandise such as cooking stoves, bicycles, smartphones and water tanks. Customers who have paid off their solar system, can acquire these additional products, and pay for them in the same way as if they are paying their lighting. If they cease payments, their lights get turned off.

TEARING UP THE RULE BOOK

"The main objective for any business in the world is to hire excellent people. If you can do that, everything else comes easy," says Moore. "It remains a challenge, though, which is not unique to M-KOPA." What is unique is that the company operates in a new industry without an existing talent pool. "We've had to go fishing for top employees in adjacent industries. Everybody who joined us tore up the rule book and relearnt everything," he says. "Naturally, this took time."

It's not all completely foreign, though, as the company is essentially a financial services business with a large balance sheet and loan book. "Our product may be different but the methodology isn't all that different," he says. "From a credit perspective, we look for people with banking and micro-financing backgrounds."

Rural customers are hard to reach due to poor transport infrastructure and the fact that they are dispersed over large areas. To overcome this challenge, M-KOPA relies on hundreds of direct sales representatives (DSRs) to sell its solar systems to customers in remote villages. After the solar systems have been manufactured, they are transported to the M-KOPA retail outlets scattered across major towns. It is here that the DSRs collect the kits and take them deeper into the villages where the real market lies.

Initially, M-KOPA relied on existing vendors and shops to sell its solar systems, but changed tack after realising this model was not conducive for rapid growth. Its network of DSRs has helped M-KOPA solve the common challenge of last-mile distribution which plagues many businesses trying to distribute goods and services to Africa's rural communities.

"Having units sit in a store on a shelf was not as productive as getting the product to the people so that they can see, touch and feel it. Perhaps it will one day become so popular that people would come to stores to buy it over the counter, but for now, it doesn't work that way. It's not a super simple product, nor is it a product people have seen before," says Moore.

M-KOPA's DSRs are paid on a commission basis, making on average between $150 to $200 per month. However, there are DSRs earning significantly more than this, and who treat it as a full-time job.

BUSINESS IS A MARATHON

"There's a growing up moment in any company when you don't know everybody's names anymore; not all your customers' nor all your employees', when it becomes something bigger than one or two people." That's when a different approach is called for.

To some extent it makes a business depersonalised, but a company leader has to keep it at a level where everybody is comfortable, "where people want to come to work in the morning", Moore says. For him, this has to be married with the intent of scaling up the company so that it can impact across several markets. "M-KOPA is currently working through this phase and I believe we will come out good at the other end."

Perseverance and grit are essential if you want to make it anywhere, not just in Africa. "Often, along the many points on the entrepreneurial path, it feels like success is not going to come," Moore says, "but you just keep on walking." When speaking to upcoming entrepreneurs, he always compares it to being stuck in a storm. "The worst thing you can do is sit down and stop moving. Keep pushing forward and know that eventually the storm will clear up and you will reach the other end. Every successful business is built on a lot of determination," he says. "Anybody who decides to go it alone should be ready for that. The great moments are many but so are the helluva tough ones."

Things don't become easier as a business grows, either. "It changes but it doesn't get any easier. It helps to set mental milestones – in six years the company will reach this target, this phase will be over but there will be another challenge – to carry you through. Understand that the challenges will evolve and that the main challenge is always to find the energy and the fun and the newness in it," Moore says of his experience.

"Balance yourself. You can't run a marathon if you don't get enough sleep, exercise and food. And running a new business is a marathon, not a sprint."

18.

Twapewa Kadhikwa

How one hair salon became a group of companies

By Confidence Musariri

When Twapewa Kadhikwa decided to work as an assistant in a hair salon to help pay her university fees, she had no idea that it would put her on the road to running a group of companies with interests in several sectors, including consumer goods, agribusiness, hospitality, training and property.

Kadhikwa was a second-year BCom student at the University of Namibia (UNAM) when her father began struggling to keep up with her tuition fees. She took a weekend job as a shampoo girl at a hair salon and was soon known as the hairdresser "who has natural oils from her village that boost hair growth". After hours, she went from house to house, knocking on doors to ask if anyone needed their hair done for Sunday church or a memorial service.

"In my third year, I asked my father not to pay for my tuition fees anymore. He thought I was dropping out and was shocked when he heard that I had enough money to pay my own study fees," she recalls.

By the end of 2002, a year after finishing university, she had a solid base of clients and established her own salon from a rented house in Katutura, a large township in Namibia's capital Windhoek.

Despite her success as a hairdresser, her family and friends still had a hard time understanding her entrepreneurial ambitions. "They laughed at me for being a hairdresser and mocked me for not joining the corporate sector. Having a degree and a job had greater status than being an entrepreneur. People would rather attend my graduation ceremony than come to the opening party for my salon."

COMMERCIALISING THE MARULA FRUIT

The idea of making natural haircare and beauty products first came to her when she noticed that her clients' hair would sometimes break despite using the mainstream haircare products. She started bringing oil extracted from the fruit of the marula tree, which grows abundantly in northern Namibia where she hails from, to the salon. Marula oil is believed to nourish hair and promote hair growth. It was a hit with her clients.

In the same year that she got her degree she attended a training course in South Africa to learn how to make cosmetics and was provided with some raw materials needed for production. Her first range consisted of a moisturiser, hair-braid spray and petroleum jelly made with marula and mongongo oil. She called her brand Pewa, a shortened version of her name, Twapewa.

By setting up small women's cooperatives in the north of the country, she ensured a steady supply of raw materials for Pewa and created a lifeline for the women in an area where work is scarce. In addition to salons, Kadhikwa sold her products to retailers and wholesalers. She even exported some.

Soon she was able to buy the building from where she had

been operating her salon. "I was growing up a little faster than I expected," she says. "I was missing out on a lot of stuff associated with being in your early twenties. Where others went to clubs and searched for the latest music, I sought to increase my marula stock and keep the business viable," she recalls.

A LEAP OF FAITH INTO THE RESTAURANT TRADE

From hair and beauty products to a restaurant is a big leap but not when you consider that marula oil, on which Pewa was built, comes in a cosmetic grade and a food grade and has many health benefits. To explore the culinary potential of the oil while bringing traditional Namibian cooking back into favour, she opened a restaurant.

The restaurant is part of the Xwama Cultural Village, which she and her husband, Erastus, established in 2008 in Katutura, a year after they married. At the time, there were hardly any traditional restaurants in and around Windhoek and no shortage of sceptics. "Before Xwama opened, the only traditional food you could find was served on old newspapers at open market stalls that were not very hygienic. We wanted to take traditional food up a notch and add value to our culture to dispel the belief that only macaroni and pizza are good enough for our people," Kadhikwa says.

"I also wanted to cater to the city's emerging middle class who did not want to eat pizza every day and longed for traditional foods found only in the villages, far from the fast Windhoek life. In Windhoek they were mostly exposed to fast food. I was convinced that during the 365 days between the one Christmas and the next – the only time many of them went home – they would long for their culture and the food they ate at home."

Xwama therefore serves traditional dishes such as bean soup, goat's head and dry game in hand-carved wooden bowls and plates. Waitresses kneel in the traditional form of respect when they present the food. "In China, they don't serve you Namibian food but Chinese food. It's the same everywhere in the world. We combine first-class service with traditional food at Xwama. We also have a duty to remind people of their identity through food," she says.

TEETHING PAINS

On the surface it may look as if success came easy to her but Kadhikwa says the challenges never cease. Soon after opening the restaurant, she realised that never having been to a hospitality school herself was a major drawback. So she started the Xwama School of Hospitality, a school where young people are trained in waitressing, bartending, housekeeping, food preparation and front-office management. "It was difficult to learn on the go in an area that was alien to me. It taught me to appreciate and understand the value of skills and so we opened the school."

It didn't help that many doubted whether the restaurant would work. "Back then, no one wanted to invest in Katutura. The banks would not fund me because Katutura was seen to be cursed and rotting with poverty. To open a restaurant in such an area was considered ill-advised. I had to overcome the label of being a township restaurant when people preferred to go to KFC, Wimpy or Spur. I was selling traditional meat, for goodness sake. Our own brothers and sisters mocked me for selling mopane worms, goat's head and traditional beer. The odds were against me."

She tells how one top bank rejected her loan request after

evaluating her business. "They had never seen a business like that in a place like that, and could not imagine it would thrive. The system was against me; I could not apply for a loan to sell mopane worms. To them, it is a dirty product for grandmothers in rural areas. It was tough.

"It is only now that I can talk about the mistakes I made and the challenges I faced in all respects: planning the business, HR management, administration, marketing and sales, operation, leadership and organisational development."

One such mistake was accepting a loan out of desperation. After many of her loan applications were rejected, one bank agreed to lend her money but it was less than the amount she needed. "I wanted money to buy machinery to manufacture my Pewa products and I requested N$400 000 in 2005. The bank only approved N$250 000. I should not have taken that money. Not having enough money limited my production capacity. They gave me less than I needed and kept me on a leash to settle the loan. I regret that move. I hate paying instalments to this day."

MOVING DOWN THE VALUE CHAIN

The local marathon chicken (also called the village chicken) on Xwama's menu was hugely popular but clients, and Kadhikwa, weren't too happy about the erratic availability due to an irregular supply. When the couple were given the chance to buy a poultry farm in 2013, they jumped at the opportunity.

"When Erastus pointed out that we risk losing customers if chicken continues to be in short supply, we either had to find a firm supplier or farm the breed of chickens needed ourselves. At that point, no one was interested in being our critical supply partner, so we decided to open the chicken farm," explains Kadhikwa.

Kadhikwa Chicken Farming has turned into an independent business which operates at a full capacity of 8 000 birds. It supplies the Xwama restaurant as well as most of Windhoek's restaurants and supermarkets, and also exports frozen chicken. To reach this level, Kadhikwa had to be hands-on and jokes that it was the first time she had to manage something other than people.

There were times when they lost a 100 or more chickens to Newcastle disease in less than a fortnight, but she never gave up. Instead, she employed synchronised hatching, a system whereby the first hen to become broody is given one dummy egg to sit on. As the others become broody, they are each given a dummy egg too and only when all of them are ready, are the dummy eggs taken away. This way, they lay at the same time and all the chicks hatch on the same day, making it easy to vaccinate them. Yet again it was a case of learning on the go.

With her husband focused on the chicken farm, the Kadhikwas put all their operations into one entity, Kadhikwa Group of Companies (KGC), of which they are the chairpersons. The group employs 190 full-time employees, including the hairdresser who started with Kadhikwa when she was at university, who now manages the first salon she had opened.

FAILURE NOT AN OPTION

Kadhikwa calls herself an entrepreneurship activist and sees it as the key to accelerating Africa's economic development, since she considers policies and some leaders to have failed in this regard. She speaks passionately about this: "If we can advance the culture of entrepreneurship, our people will flourish, not only in Africa, but they will also be able to operate beyond the continent. I am demanding that other successful businesspeople become involved. If you are successful, why are you not sharing your 'recipe' with young people who can learn from you? Namibia sits with 2.6 million people and 43 per cent of them are unemployed; 70 per cent of our unemployed people are youth. We are mandated to impact our generation. It is not a hobby; it is an entrepreneurship mandate."

Experience has taught her it's important to be open-minded. "Stay laser focused on solutions but consider and evaluate myriad ways to achieve them. Be open to readjusting, recalibrating and relaunching. Do not make your business about you. When you are sick, the business should not become sick too. Otherwise, when you die, the business will die too. That is the wrong formula. Your business should evolve from being a one-man show to a generational business."

This is one of the reasons KGC has begun to look further afield and she mentions Ghana, Kenya, China and India. She states, "Namibia is not doing well in export-driven areas such as mining, agriculture and fisheries. We have to invest in the land in order to diversify. KGC is now considering West Africa and Asian markets with our agriculture portfolio. We have engaged an Israeli company to conduct a feasibility study and are almost there. When the president of the African Development Bank, Akinwumi Adesina, was hosted for dinner at Xwama, he said the next billionaire in Africa will come from agriculture. I think he meant to say Xwama, not Africa. I felt he was talking about me."

Kadhikwa's determination to become financially independent was a major factor in her success as an entrepreneur. "It was the lure of financial freedom and the challenge of mapping my own destiny while determining the pace of my life that pulled me into business. I never had a back-up, no insurance, no pension, no investment plan, but I told myself I would not fail. I never contemplated failure. I had to survive. The only option was to go."

She believes that too many people who have entrepreneurial skills are numbed by fear of failure. "The other evening I was alone in my room and discovered a snake in the room. Instinctively, I killed it, drank a coffee and tucked myself into bed. That is when I learnt something about myself – I'm not perfect, but I do not fear anything."

19.

Jacques de Vos
Growing a high-impact tech business one problem statement at a time

By Jeanette Clark

Jacques de Vos's mind is wired according to mathematical and engineering principles. When he speaks, it is as if he's trying to balance an equation and solve for the missing variable. Most of his comments and arguments can be translated into a mathematical problem statement with ease.

Technology + y = productive societies (solve for *y*)

Or:

If *a* is equal to the opportunity that is present when applying technology, then:

Technology x Scandinavia = 2a vs *Technology x Africa = 5a + systemic change*

"I am a mathematician in the way I think about things," he says matter-of-factly when explaining the principles on which he bases his business decisions. This is probably because the

37-year-old CEO of South African-based technology and advisory firm Mezzanine was born and raised to be an engineer.

"My grandfather and his brothers were engineers or engineering professors. My dad and his five brothers were all engineers. Both my brothers are engineers. My cousins are engineers," he says. Having grown up in a family where discussions around the dinner table were always about building bridges, or power stations or steel factories, it was inevitable that he would enrol to study engineering at Stellenbosch University in South Africa after high school.

Shortly after graduating, De Vos realised that he could not, however, with any conviction, call himself an engineer. "My childhood was all play – fun and games. I cannot really recall doing any hard work, not even during the first four years of university. I was lucky. I could cram, write an exam and pass, but when I finished my degree I could not remember a thing. I could not present myself at that stage as an engineer and therefore decided to do my master's degree," De Vos remembers. "It forced me to apply my mind and think about what I wanted to do."

His decision on the next step was in part based on advice he had received from his father: whatever you want to do, start as early as possible. "Because the longer you wait, for example, to start a business, the greater the opportunity cost. If you're fresh out of university, having lived like a tramp for a couple of years, continuing to live like one for another couple of years while establishing your business is not a big deal. If you are married and have four children, though, it is almost impossible."

The topic of his electrical and electronic engineering master's thesis, which he completed in 2005, pointed the way: he had wanted to design an automated algorithm that could help primary-care physicians to screen and diagnose children with possible heart problems.

The following year he co-founded a technology company, GeoMed, with fellow engineer Thys Cronje. Their vision was to develop medical devices and healthcare solutions for emerging markets and together they launched the SensiCardiac device which processes the digitally recorded sound of a heartbeat through intelligent algorithms to accurately identify and diagnose heart problems.

FIND A WAY TO MAKE TOUGH DECISIONS

Three years later, they had created two spin-off companies. One, Diacoustic Medical Devices, focused on commercialising De Vos's master's research and the other, GIH, developed software to help tuberculosis and HIV/Aids patients to adhere to their treatment.

Valuable lessons were learnt in the process of taking these two concepts to market. "You need to tick all three value-creation boxes if you want to build a business. You have to create value by developing a solution to a problem. But that is not enough. You also have to be able to deliver that value cost-effectively to your target audience. And then you have to be able to capture the value you have created – you must be able to monetise it and derive an income from it."

The founders also learnt that it was a lot easier to distribute and capture value in resource-limited countries if you have a software-focused business. "As opposed to having a hardware-focused business where you physically manufacture something, software allows you to leverage the principles of a digital and connected world; it is free, it is perfect, and it is instant," De Vos explains.

To pay the bills during this start-up phase and to fund the development of more projects and potential spin-offs, GeoMed continued to do consultation work for clients such as the South African Medical Research Council; various development funders, such as USAID; and mobile-technology companies, like MTN, Vodafone and Nokia.

"At the time, we viewed GeoMed as an incubator," says De Vos. "We based the model on the Living Lab concept we saw in Helsinki while we were consulting at Nokia and Vodafone on matters such as the use of mobile technology for assisted living." Living Labs – first touted in Europe and specifically the Nordic countries in 2006 – are user-centred, open, innovation ecosystems where research and innovation are integrated into real communities and settings. In this way, a proposed innovation solution has the end user as its focus from the very beginning, which ensures that it will succeed when implemented.

De Vos refers to the moment which led to his decision to walk away from the medical-devices field and focus on his current company, Mezzanine, as the "Oscar moment". It happened in 2010 in the seaside town of Kleinmond during a strategy session attended by all the business partners and facilitated by Stephan Lamprecht, a trusted friend and business consultant.

"At the time we had roughly 10 projects in GeoMed and the two spin-off companies, which operated as standalone businesses. I was executively responsible for GIH. We were discussing the future of GeoMed and at around two o'clock in the morning, we came to the conclusion that if we wanted to be successful, we had to pick only one project. We had to pick an 'Oscar' project."

As a result, the majority of the 10 projects were terminated to allow them to achieve this focus. De Vos resigned from GIH and began working on building and developing the chosen project that would ultimately, 12 months later in October 2011, lead to the founding of Mezzanine.

Mezzanine is a technology and advisory company with the slogan "Creating productive societies". It enters into partnerships with governments, business owners, development agencies and subject experts to leverage digital capabilities to make a difference in people's lives. By building platforms and harnessing the opportunities offered by mobile technology, it provides healthcare and agriculture solutions in South Africa, Nigeria, Zambia, Mozambique, Tanzania, Ghana and Kenya.

AitaHealth, one of its solutions, is an app used by community health workers to register all members in a household and screen, flag, educate, refer and schedule follow-up tasks for them, all via smartphone. In this way, it helps with disease prevention and early detection, and promotes community health. mVaccination is a mobile app, too, and is used by clinic workers to record children on a database and send each one's caregiver SMS notifications of scheduled appointments. It also tracks vaccine stock levels and fridge temperatures to ensure safe storage. In June 2018, mVaccination was selected by the Global Alliance for Vaccines and Immunisation (GAVI) as one of 11 finalist innovations, thus receiving international recognition for the impact it could have.

Another product is Connected Farmer, an enterprise mobile-enabled solution, which connects agribusinesses and smallholder farmers by digitising the value chain. In the education field, the School Management System allows more than 12 000 schools in South Africa and Nigeria to report incidents, monitor priority programmes, like school feeding programmes, and submit enrolment and attendance statistics via their phones.

In 2012, Vodacom, one of the major telecoms players in Africa, took up a majority share in Mezzanine. The Kleinmond group's Oscar project had begun to pay off. De Vos calls the two years between making the decision to leave the security of his managing position at GIH to the time that the transaction with Vodacom became a reality, "two years of hell".

"You have to talk to my wife to understand exactly how difficult this transition period was," he says openly. They moved towns twice and lived with his in-laws for more than a year. They also had their first two children. "In the midst of all this turmoil and change, I decided to leave the security of a paid job."

He believes having a partner who supports you and buys into your dream is critical if you are to succeed on your entrepreneurial journey. "There are no guarantees, no estimated time of arrival. You basically get in the car and say: 'This is the idea and I don't know if we have enough gas in the tank to get where we are hoping to go. Are you in or are you out?'"

ATTRACTING AND KEEPING THE RIGHT PEOPLE

One of his biggest fears is losing important team members. This was a particular concern in the early days. "In the beginning you don't have the means to establish redundancies. If you lose just one vital team member in the first three or four years, you are in trouble; basically you are looking at closing the business."

Today, Mezzanine has a strong team of more than 50 employees, but recruitment and retention remain challenges as young, tech-savvy, millennial developers continuously seek new opportunities. Because they are in short supply, such employees are continually being headhunted and lured with better salary offers. As a result, in 2015 and especially in 2016, Mezzanine struggled with high staff turnover. "We really had to revisit our approach. We had to establish an environment that is more conducive to co-creation and development that would resonate with the employees we want to attract and keep," De Vos says. Their recruitment approach now is to find people who are first and foremost interested in the reason behind Mezzanine's operations – the *why* rather than the *what* or *how*.

"We are not playing in a sexy space," he says, referring to the bitcoins and blockchains of the world; the ones vying to become the next big thing. "For example, we built a system that makes sure that kids get their daily meals at school. If that doesn't speak to you, you will find it hard to work on the project for three years and not get bored," he states.

The culture change has been so successful that Mezzanine now offers to house the development teams of multinationals which are struggling to establish a culture that appeals to developers and coders, at the Mezzanine premises.

LOCK DOWN YOUR PRINCIPLES AND STICK TO THEM

Doing business in Africa and in a highly disruptable industry means there will always be tough decisions to make.

De Vos says there are some attributes that are beneficial to an entrepreneur. "You should definitely not be risk averse," he comments. He also believes that having a set of principles which speeds up the decision-making process when faced with difficult choices has helped him to achieve success.

"I don't overthink and overanalyse. I use gut feel; you can probably even say I am gung-ho." In the end, though, he bases all his decisions on a framework and foundation of principles that run from his deepest belief systems through to his personal life and finally to his business.

The first is co-creation, not because it happens to be one of the business management buzzwords of the year, but because it is a valuable tool in risk mitigation in his line of business.

"Designing and developing a new proposition are not things you do in a lab. Ultimately the answer to a problem is always embedded in the ecosystem experiencing the problem," he says. "Working with multinationals in Africa has taught us that there is a gap between what head office knows and understands about the operations and the on-the-ground realities. It is such a big problem that, as a starting point in any new discussion, we say that we expect there to be a gap between the two. We mitigate this risk by introducing co-creation across all levels," De Vos explains.

End-to-end stakeholder representation + co-creation = success

Secondly, the team at Mezzanine has learnt to approach problem statements incrementally and to first attack elements with low complexity and high value.

"As an engineer, complexity to some extent is attractive. We have learnt, unfortunately only relatively recently, that we should take off our engineering hats and focus on low complexity, high-value opportunities," De Vos says. This is partly because the problems encountered in resource-scarce countries such as Tanzania and Mozambique go beyond the technical. Political considerations, commercial and socio-economic challenges, as well as logistics, all come into play.

"We've learnt to start with one choke point and once we've

solved that problem, we move on. In time, all these stepping stone solutions become a comprehensive solution."

Systemic change = solution(1) + solution(2) +… + solution(n), where *n* equals the number of choke points

Saying no is not something that comes naturally to De Vos. It is something he had to learn. "When it comes to solving problems, I am a bit of a people pleaser. If I know I can do something, I almost feel obliged or responsible to do it. There are many opportunities and a lot of buzz out there, but to be successful as a business, I personally and we as a company should remain focused. We want to solve system-level problems in Africa. So, whenever we engage in an opportunity, we have to be sure that we have the appetite and the capacity to engage for three to five years."

Focus = saying no

The fourth principle he lives and works by is the importance of trusted relationships. "I will walk away from an opportunity if I get the sense that we are not in a position where there is trust," De Vos says. For him, the first step in developing trust in a professional environment is to make sure your client feels and sees that solving the problem matters to you.

"This trust has to be external as well as internal and speaks to the culture in our company too. We always work in teams. We never work as individuals. There is no one person who is amazing and who can do everything, but as a team, we are amazing and can do everything."

Opportunity – trusted relationship ≠ true opportunity

The final and most important principle is the theory of value creation and having an impact. If a solution does not have a clear value proposition and supporting business case (albeit one with risk and assumptions built into it) that allow it to be scaled and sustained, then it's not worth pursuing. "This stems from our belief that what we do should have an impact. To have an impact, you need to develop something that holds a tangible benefit for at least 50 per cent of the people you deliver the product or service to."

For Mezzanine, a technological innovation only has an impact if people and households derive a real benefit from it and if it helps to better their quality of life.

Innovation + >50 per cent impact for economic unit = economic value

"My belief is that we are here to have an external impact. If you are only here for x number of days, you have to ask yourself how to translate that time into the greatest benefit – what will be the most productive use of your time? That is where technology really is a wonderful multiplier," he says, talking about his commitment to making a difference in Africa and playing his part to ensure the continent participates in the Fourth Industrial Revolution.

"What often gets to me is how self-centred people can be. I am not judging, but without a purpose and a belief, someone's world becomes noticeably smaller," he says.

NO SUCH THING AS A FINISH LINE

Every story has a beginning, middle and end, or so traditional storytelling would have us believe. De Vos's entrepreneurial journey is not that linear. There have been several cycles of beginnings, middles and endings.

He has had to find it in himself over and over again to motivate his teams when they needed to rework, regroup and find a new approach. Has there ever been a moment when he just could not find it in himself to be enthusiastic about another cycle or restart?

"No," he states honestly. "I've never had to motivate myself that way. It's just there. Of course, I sometimes go to bed at night tired and *gatvol* (fed-up)," he admits. "But the next morning I get up and somehow I have the energy to do it.

"There is always something on the horizon. You have never arrived. There isn't such a thing as a finishing line. There is always something more: a new country, a new product. That is the ongoing perpetual motivator."

So: *Technology + y = productive societies* (solve for y)

For Jacques de Vos, y = *impact*.

Always.

.

20.

Nana Akua Birmeh

Architect breaking glass ceilings in Ghana

By Kwasi Gyamfi Asiedu

"As an architect, you can't sit in a space without assessing everything you see and sometimes thinking 'that window shouldn't have been there and this door should have been swinging in that direction'," Nana Akua Birmeh says, and laughs: "It's strange to think I almost didn't become the architectural snob that I am today."

If it wasn't for Birmeh's mother, she would not have gone to architecture school. Birmeh and her father had conspired for her to study visual arts at high school without her mother's knowledge, knowing full well that she would not approve, as she did not believe there were viable careers for artists. After a family friend told her that a visual arts qualification could also lead to a career in architecture, Birmeh's mother relented, on condition that she study architecture at university.

"So, I didn't really have a choice. I ventured into architecture having no clue what it was. Literally, no clue. I had never met an architect in my life," she says.

Seventeen years down the line, Birmeh is happy that her mother had insisted, as she enjoyed architecture school immensely. "Mother knows best," she jokes. Today, Mrs

Oppong's presence can be felt in her daughter's office at ArchXenus, her architecture firm, in Ghana's capital Accra. "That was the base of my mother's sewing machine," says Birmeh and points to the green plinth that forms the base of her glass-topped desk. Aside from being her way of paying homage to her mother, the 36-year-old ArchXenus CEO says the base inspires her when she is sketching the next home or office for a client somewhere in Ghana.

Ultimately, the driving motivation for starting her own company was her own desire to be a mother and still be an architect, too. When she realised that the firm she was working for was not suited to accommodate maternity, motherhood and family life, she gathered her life savings and started out on her own in 2008. First, she worked freelance from home. As her workload increased, she employed more and more architects until they outgrew her home and had to move to an office.

In 2011, ArchXenus was born; taking the *arch* of architecture and combining it with *xenos*, the Greek word for *different* or *unique*, to form the company name. At the same time, Birmeh's eldest son, Jon-Wamal, was born and often was present during those early days, slumbering in his cot beside his mother's desk or demanding a break in client meetings to breastfeed. Another two sons and a daughter later, the company is Ghana's largest homegrown architecture firm with a staff averaging 50, which includes 23 architects.

In the beginning, many clients were unsure of this new firm and Birmeh says, "For many, the stereotype of an architect is old and male. And we were young women who said we could design their homes, which they were spending their life savings on."

PIONEERING A NEW BUILDING STYLE

As a result, jobs were few and far between and Ghana's laws – which limit how much an architect may charge – hampered ArchXenus's profitability. Only once Birmeh "cracked the code", one that worked particularly well for residential apartment blocks and townhouse complexes, around the same time that Accra's construction boom began, did things look up for ArchXenus. The cranes and new high-rise apartments which dot the city's skyline are signs of the ever-increasing contribution construction is making to the Ghanaian economy. In 2017, the industry contributed 13.7 per cent of the country's GDP, according to the Ghana Statistical Service, compared to 5.7 per cent in 2006.

Birmeh speaks with pride of her firm's work to pioneer a new building style in Ghana; one that eschews elaborate aesthetics just for the sake of it. "I come from a school of thought that focuses on functionality and finding the aesthetics, the beauty, in the pure function of a building." Being at the intersection of functional design and a thriving construction industry "has been very rewarding", she says. In 2014, ArchXenus turned a profit and hasn't looked back since. In 2017 alone, the firm designed 53 projects with a total budget of about $140 million.

Birmeh had to find a way around another legal hurdle. Architecture firms, like law firms and private attorneys, are not allowed to advertise or market their services in Ghana. Her response was to let her buildings do the advertising for them.

"Isn't a building a far bigger billboard than any other? I want people to drive by a building or visit a place and be compelled to ask, 'Who designed this?' If someone wants to, they will fish you out wherever you are." For Birmeh, that is the best path to success for entrepreneurs, regardless of the sector they're in or whether they're allowed to advertise or not. "To attract new clients, the fundamental thing is the product. You can hire the best ad agency in the world, but if what you offer is no good, the result of the advertising effort will be nil. Let your work speak for itself.

"At ArchXenus, we treat every project that comes to us like the World Cup. It could be a bathroom extension or a billion-dollar project, both get the same heart, the same dedication and the same level of creativity. We do everything with 100 per cent dedication," says Birmeh.

Smaller residential jobs have been picking up at the firm. A home, says Birmeh, is the largest investment most people will make in their lives, but many Ghanaians don't contract architects when building theirs. At best, they get a local draughts-man to quickly draw up a plan and in no time masons are on site and laying blocks. In the end, she says, they are left with a structure that has no personality or soul, a space they cannot connect with and truly enjoy. "When an architect has designed a home, it is still going to be built block by block just like any other building, but the difference is that somebody has sat down to think and feel the space first; to visualise and experience it."

Birmeh doesn't like the word "challenges". "There are times when we have to chase clients to pay up and we have abandoned a couple of projects after spending days and nights thinking and drawing because the client didn't have the money to continue with it. Sometimes we have to scale down aspects of a design to fit a client's revised budget and, as an artist, that is very unpleasant to do. All these things happen but I choose not to call them challenges.

"Nothing is ever wasted. Sometimes someone comes to us with a project which looks good and we give it our all, as always, but it doesn't go through. Often, some months down the line, we take inspiration from that abandoned design for a new viable project." As a devout Christian, Birmeh believes everything happens for a reason, even if that reason only manifests months or even years later.

Not that some of the setbacks haven't been the result of her mistakes. "Not supervising a construction site always turns out bad. We have now made it a general rule that when a client asks us to design a building for them, they at the same time agree that we supervise the construction. Or else we won't do it."

DOING YOUR OWN THING DOESN'T MEAN DOING IT ALONE

Having to make tough business decisions and having the tenacity to stick to them are the reasons being an entrepreneur is not for everyone, she says.

"The popular narrative is: don't work for someone, quit your nine-to-five and do your own thing, be your own boss. As a result, people start a business without passion, without conviction, without any new ideas to differentiate themselves. That is why they bow out when they hit the first small stumbling blocks. There is a belief that you won't be considered successful if you're not doing your own thing. My advice is that you can still be successful in your field at a company you didn't start yourself."

For Birmeh, being an entrepreneur meant having to embrace selflessness. "Everything you do reaches beyond yourself and it takes every shred of selfishness away. You have to make business decisions that often go beyond and against your personal interests and preferences. Even when you want to go in one direction, you have to refrain and go in another that will be better for the business, even if you hate it."

Running a business also teaches you about your own shortcomings. "There is only so much you can do yourself. My skills end at a certain point. I can't do everything. All of us at ArchXenus bring our own strengths so that our battleship is better prepared when we face our opposition. Our process is very collaborative and the outcome is not only my doing.

"You need help with managing all the correspondence, budgets, payments. One person can't do it all. Yet many people do everything themselves to live up to the image of a superhero-entrepreneur who built a successful business all on their own. In those cases, either the product or management will suffer. Either way, you won't have the best possible outcome."

Of her leadership style, Birmeh says simply: "It comes straight from the heart, from a place of empathy" – the kind of empathy that draws on her own work experience before starting her firm. At ArchXenus, Birmeh makes sure that being a parent and having a job are not mutually exclusive. "People shouldn't have to choose between having a fulfilling career and having a family," she says. It is not unusual to see small children running around their offices with a nanny hot on their heels. She brought in a bouncy castle for the little ones and created a dedicated homework space for the older children.

The working relationships are mostly horizontal, probably because she and many of her employees fall within the same age gap – or at least, they were, she says, and tells of a new employee who recently called her "auntie"!

LOOKING BEYOND THE HERE AND THE NOW

When seeing her contemporaries who are freelancing – "they have more money, better cars, more everything" – she often thinks that could have been her, too. "Had I chosen that path though, it would have meant that my work and contribution would end the day I stopped working. I am looking at leaving a legacy."

For one, Birmeh wants to revolutionise the architectural practice in Ghana. She describes the typical career path of an architect in Ghana as follows: "You go through six years of hard labour in school and finish, and then you start looking for a practising architect to follow, literally. Half the time you won't join an establishment with a clear future but just an architect doing their thing. When you've gathered some skills, you strike out on your own and then others come to learn from you before going off to do their own thing.

"That is why we don't have any architectural firm in Ghana that has outlived its founder. It is sad. I want ArchXenus to be different, to outlive me and the people working here. Our children's children should be able to see a thriving company that was built on the hard work of their mothers' mothers and fathers' fathers."

As a result, Birmeh toils to ensure that ArchXenus's office is inclusive. "I make sure that everyone, from the cleaner to a partner, feels that they own this place. Our futures are tied together. Every employee has to take ownership of what happens in the business. From day one, this is drummed into new team members. Some may align with the vision and others may not but everyone is invited to connect in this way."

Building a legacy is a big task and Birmeh is well aware

that ArchXenus will have to do bigger things and do more than high-end townhouses in Accra to realise this. Although they have designed a new airport in central Ghana, and have a shopping mall in the port city of Tema and a children's centre in Accra lined up, she is already talking about going bigger. Two years ago, ArchXenus began bidding for projects outside the country, most of which are done by submitting anonymous tenders.

"We realised a lot of the notable architectural offices in the world thrive on international tenders. By the time a tender is put out, bidders know the project is secure, that it has its funding, that it has everything in place. When you win, it is usually against some of the biggest names in the business, which gives you a certain level of credibility.

"Every year, we pick one international project and pitch a design," she says. They have submitted designs for the Lima Art Museum in Peru in 2016 and for Dar Al-Uloum, a public library in Sakaka in Saudi Arabia, in 2017. They have yet to be successful with a bid but Birmeh, "being an eternal optimist", believes that things will start happening as long as they keep bidding.

"In 10 years' time, I hope we will be a household name in Ghana and all over the world just like Bjarke Ingles, Norman Foster and my role model Zaha Hadid." To do this, Birmeh is focusing on the one thing she knows best: "The product, which in my industry is unique design."

21.

Nelly Tuikong

Kenyan beauty brand taking on global behemoths

By Dinfin Mulupi & Jaco Maritz

"I'm proud of having built a local cosmetics brand that is competing neck and neck with international companies in the market. Right now, I can walk into a beauty shop and my stand is next to the giants, such as Revlon and Maybelline. It is incredible."

So says Nelly Tuikong, founder and executive director of Pauline Cosmetics. The Kenyan company, named after Tuikong's mother, produces a range of beauty products such as lipstick, eye shadow and makeup brushes that retail throughout the country and is slowly gaining traction in Uganda and Rwanda.

Looking back on her journey, Tuikong, now in her early thirties, says she had to learn everything about being a businessperson from scratch. "Entrepreneurship is like having your first baby. You have people and books telling you what to do but when that baby shows up, you have no clue what to do.

"That said, in a way I'm glad I didn't start out with set assumptions and that I figured it out as I went along. Many people have been burnt by having assumptions on how business in Africa works, only to see their ventures collapse. Whatever you read in international case studies or business books doesn't necessarily apply to rural Kenya," she explains.

Tuikong grew up in the western part of the country, living a typical Kenyan middle-class lifestyle. But around the age of 10, her situation suddenly took a turn for the worse when her father lost his job and the family had to rely on her mother's income as a nurse. Upon completing high school, Tuikong's options to study further were limited due to a lack of finances and she went to stay with a family member in the city of Eldoret.

After taking on several low-paying casual jobs, she ended up working at a hospital where she had to care for abandoned babies. The experience stimulated an interest in healthcare and she decided to follow in her mother's footsteps and become a nurse. However, all three of her applications to medical training institutions were rejected.

As one door closed, another opened. At the hospital she met an American couple, Stephen and Judy Leapman, who were in Kenya to do volunteer work. Tuikong became friends with the family and joined them on an excursion to the town of Kitale, during which they discussed her career ambitions. About two weeks after the trip, Judy pulled her aside one day and announced that the family wanted to sponsor her to study nursing in the United States.

"My life was turned around; they handed me a clean slate," Tuikong later told radio and TV talk-show host Amina Abdi Rabar.

FROM NURSE TO ENTREPRENEUR

It was in her final year of studies that the entrepreneurship bug bit and Tuikong began thinking of developing her own beauty brand: "I saw someone had launched a new cosmetics line in the States and thought, 'Who needs another product in this market?' There are hundreds of makeup brands in the US but I somehow knew the new company would probably be a success. Then it struck me, 'What about Africa?' There was a gap in the colour-cosmetics market. I began entertaining the idea and soon could not shake it off."

It took her four years – from 2009 until 2013 – to go from experimenting with making lip gloss in her kitchen to launching Pauline Cosmetics. She admits to facing internal struggles because she left nursing behind to start a business. Even after moving back to Kenya in 2011, she took a job in clinical research and worked on her venture in her free time. She kept her business a secret from most of those around her.

"I felt like a fraud. People had invested in me to go to school and I felt as if I was betraying them. When I was around people in the medical community, I would feel extremely guilty. I felt that I was supposed to help people and save lives, yet I had the desire to start my own business and make profits," she says.

In 2013, she imported her first shipment from Asia and stored the products in a spare room in her house. At that stage, Pauline Cosmetics was unknown in the Kenyan market. She now admits that it had been a mistake to import products before knowing how, and to whom, she was going to sell them.

"I was running out of money and couldn't afford a fancy launch. Eventually, I had to give away almost half the products because they were coming to the end of their shelf life. I was selling items at throwaway prices just to recoup my initial investment."

Although she believed Kenya's beauty and cosmetics industry was in for a major change, the market simply wasn't yet ready. "People were still very conservative and the avenues for selling new products were limited. It wasn't like today when people are more adventurous with makeup. But I knew the economy would grow, that the middle class would swell and there would be extra income to spend on luxury items like makeup. Another factor I didn't predict was how the popularity of social media would boost the beauty industry as a whole, particularly the selfie trend that hit Kenya around 2015. It wasn't that long ago but a lot has changed since 2013. I came in a bit too early but early enough to appreciate the industry's journey.

"All along I had speculated that it could be a big market. I knew of another Kenyan cosmetics brand which was under development and it gave me the validation I needed. International brands were also expanding into Africa. But when my products landed, that shift had not yet happened," Tuikong explains.

A STEEP LEARNING CURVE

All Pauline Cosmetics products are manufactured abroad, mostly in China and Taiwan. However, importing and working with overseas manufacturers were often frustrating.

"At one point I had to wire money to a factory in Asia but I was living in Kenya and the money was in my bank account in the United States. I asked a friend in America to wire the money from her account with the agreement that I'd refund her. When her account was frozen because the authorities thought she was offshoring money from the US to China, I had to prove that the money was going to a legitimate party in Asia. It was unbelievably frustrating."

When asked about the toughest situation she's found herself in as a business owner, Tuikong tells of the day she went to the port in Mombasa, about 500km from the capital Nairobi, to clear her goods at customs. She had received documentation demanding double the amount in import duties she normally pays. At the Kenya Revenue Authority offices in Nairobi, she was told that she had to go to the port herself to get the amount reduced.

"I travelled to Mombasa. When I eventually gained access to the port area, which wasn't easy, I was surrounded by several big sweaty men in wife beaters clearing cargo for East Africa. There were hardly any women around. I walked in wearing a dress and was shown to the commissioner's office. There were about 20 people waiting to talk to him, a very powerful man, and I had no idea whether he would grant me an audience. I arrived at 9am and had to wait until 5pm to see him.

"When I eventually got to speak to him, he was like, 'Yeah, what's going on?' and said that he was in a hurry to leave. After explaining my situation, he agreed to have my entire consignment re-evaluated. It meant I had to stay at the port another five days. However, they did do the re-evaluation, and I paid what I was supposed to pay. It was a crazy week but it makes for a good story."

BUILDING A RETAIL PRESENCE

Pauline Cosmetics is predominantly sold by beauty shops and pharmacies. Tuikong doesn't yet supply mainstream supermarkets because of their unfavourable payment terms. Kenya's retail sector is highly fragmented and comprises thousands of independent shops. To make it profitable, brands have to get into many of these independents and not only the few chain stores.

Initially, she made the mistake of concentrating on expanding to new outlets and neglecting her existing stockists. Now she knows that many beauty shop owners are inexperienced entrepreneurs themselves and often need support with, for example, in-store promotions.

To help move product from the shelves, Pauline Cosmetics has its own staff stationed in some of the bigger shops. "This is a strategy I used since I noticed the spike in sales whenever we had our own salesperson in the shop pushing the products. With several brands in the market now and growing competition, I need Pauline Cosmetics representatives to help convince customers to try our products. Luckily I have built good relationships with some shop owners and managed to persuade them to have my sales staff in the shops full-time."

Whereas many global beauty houses predominantly focus on Nairobi, Tuikong has built a distribution network that reaches all corners of the country. "It's not like you can't find big brands outside Nairobi but smaller towns don't seem to be a big priority for them. I remember going into a shop in a smaller town and seeing a dirty, empty Maybelline display stand. The shop assistant said that no one from Maybelline had visited them in over a year."

In some of Kenya's smaller urban areas there is greater wealth than many realise, generated by activities such as agriculture, trading and tourism. The growth of second-tier cities has been further spurred by Kenya's 2013 roll-out of a decentralised system of governance, which divided the country into 47 counties, each with its own government and county headquarters. Since then, the county capitals have experienced an influx of government officials, which led to greater commercial activity and economic growth.

To create brand credibility, Pauline Cosmetics partnered with

Adelle Onyango, a popular Kenyan radio presenter, actress and vlogger, in May 2018 to launch a limited-edition lipstick called Limitless. Although celebrity partnerships are a popular strategy in many other parts of the world, not many makeup brands in East Africa have gone this route. "It is a different and unique way to market a product or brand and it introduced Pauline Cosmetics to people who wouldn't necessarily have given our products a chance," Tuikong explains.

She says while it is difficult to measure the impact of such initiatives, it has definitely boosted brand awareness. "We've had a lot of feedback from shop owners as well as our own sales representatives, who tell us that more people are familiar with the brand and walk into the shop and ask for Pauline Cosmetics. Whenever I interact with people and happen to mention that I own the brand, a lot more people are aware of it, which feels good. At one point we were trending on Twitter for a few hours because of this collaboration and Adelle's popularity within the media fraternity. We also had a tonne of press around it."

BUSINESS IS SWEET AND SOUR

Tuikong says her greatest weakness as an entrepreneur was being a "control freak" and "bad with delegation". However, she's become better at understanding the need to let go.

"In the past, I used to spend a week in a town to scout for business. Now I've built processes around how it is done, which allows me to send someone else to do it. I've built processes around scouting for new retailers, following up, closing a deal and what to do next when they can't close a deal.

"This *aha* moment only struck me recently, five years after launching the company. I know that people who have been in business for a long time would say, 'Duh, of course that is what you need to do,' but this is my first venture and it wasn't that obvious at the start. For instance, it hit me very clearly that I don't have to go to the bank myself every day. I can send someone else. As a result, I now have time to think about the bigger picture."

She disagrees with the conventional business wisdom that entrepreneurs should stick to their field of expertise. "I'm qualified as a critical care nurse and had zero background in beauty or business before starting out."

Tuikong has no regrets, though, about giving up a stable career in nursing to start her own business, but advises those who are only interested in making money to stick to climbing the corporate ladder.

"Sometimes I hear someone who says being an entrepreneur allows them to control their hours and to be flexible. It is absurd. There is no such thing. You don't have your own time any more. Your business becomes everything. The first years you are everything: the accountant, the social media manager, the messenger.

"Business is sweet and sour. It is the most frustrating thing you will ever do. I tend to keep my emotions under control because it is how I was raised. So when my husband sees me crying, he knows things are really bad. There are times when I need to do just that – cry, binge on some TV shows, eat a whole tub of ice cream. But then I pull myself up again the next day. It is very frustrating, but it is one of the most incredible journeys you will ever take."

22.

Dr Hend El Sherbini

From a small Egyptian family business to a
London-listed healthcare giant

By Jeanette Clark

Dr Hend El Sherbini is an optimistic pragmatist: someone who
believes the world can be made better by human effort. This
is what lies behind the hard work and commitment that have
led the soft-spoken clinical pathologist to her position as the
CEO of the London Stock Exchange-listed Integrated Diagnostics Holdings (IDH).

IDH is a consumer healthcare company with more than 4 000
employees and 400 diagnostic laboratories in Africa and the
Middle East that can perform over 1 400 internationally accred-
ited diagnostic tests. It has operations in Egypt, Jordan, Sudan
and Nigeria. In August 2018, IDH announced another expansion in a new segment to add to its portfolio of services, this
time in the field of radiology in Egypt.

"I would say that I am an optimist. It is the only way that
you can tackle things," the 49-year-old El Sherbini says while
describing her worst moment as an entrepreneur. It was when
she had to navigate the events which led to Egypt's Arab Spring
protests in 2011 and steer a growing business through the political uncertainty that followed it.

"It really impacted our work in a lot of aspects. It taught me that you have to deal with things as they come. Then things will eventually get better," she says.

ENTREPRENEURSHIP IS IN HER BLOOD

El Sherbini grew up in Cairo as the only child of a powerhouse couple. Her mother is a pathologist and her father was a surgeon. Both also had academic careers as professors at Cairo University.

"My mother has always been an extremely driven career woman," she says of Dr Moamena Kamel, today the secretary general of the Egyptian Red Crescent, a humanitarian organisation. "She was a professor at Cairo University and did her studies in France. She is a role model to me, someone who is committed to her work, very keen on the wellbeing of her patients and dedicated to delivering the highest quality service. I have her genes and was influenced by seeing the way she acts."

After high school, El Sherbini obtained a bachelor's degree in medicine and surgery, followed by a master's in clinical and chemical pathology and a doctorate in immunology (the study of immune systems) at Cairo University. She also studied at Emory University in Atlanta and worked at the Centre for Disease Control and Prevention (CDC) in the United States before returning to Cairo at the end of 2000.

Back on home soil, she was first employed as a lecturer at Cairo University before joining her mother at Moamena Kamel Laboratories, which she had started in 1979, when her daughter was 10. By the time El Sherbini joined the team in 2001, there were five laboratories with approximately 50 employees.

Returning to Cairo was not without its challenges. El

Sherbini had loved doing advanced hepatitis research at the CDC in Atlanta where she enjoyed well-resourced funding, support and facilities. In Cairo, she soon realised that there was not enough funding for the type of research she wanted to do. So she took the pragmatic decision and changed to clinical pathology (the diagnosis of disease based on laboratory analysis) and joined her mother's laboratories. "I was happy doing research at the CDC, but I also enjoyed the clinical work. I would definitely say that the lack of resources originally assisted me to make the change," she admits.

In 2004, the mother-daughter team restructured the business and renamed it Al Mokhtabar with El Sherbini as the CEO. At first, expansion was slow but, in 2007, the company undertook extensive market research to understand the needs of their clients – both physicians and patients. "Until then it didn't make sense to do much research as we were too small. One of the things our research clearly showed was that patients wanted the convenience of a lab close to them. This is why we started to expand really fast so we could be near everyone," she explains.

By 2010, the five laboratories had become 115 with 1 000 employees. The funding for this expansion was generated organically by the business and much emphasis was placed on ensuring all new facilities adhere to the same standards by obtaining international accreditation for their processes and procedures.

"Accreditation is important, not just because of the accreditation itself, but because of the process you have to undergo before receiving it," she explains. It is a long, tedious process which requires a laboratory to have all the steps and standards in place, achieve the required quality outcomes and maintain that level of quality for an extended period of time. Obtaining accreditation with the College of American Pathologists (CAP) in the United States, for example, took Al Mokhtabar two and a half years the first time they applied.

As a result of the growth and quality service, Al Mokhtabar had begun to steal some of the market share of another established laboratory in Egypt, Al Borg Laboratories. In 2010, the private equity investor group Abraaj, which had invested in Al Borg three years prior, approached El Sherbini regarding a merger. "They were not delivering in terms of targets, expansion and market share. We were eating into their market share," El Sherbini says. Al Mokhtabar also had the only CAP-accredited laboratories in Egypt.

The negotiations failed, but Abraaj approached El Sherbini again right after President Hosni Mubarak was ousted in February 2011. As they were direct competitors, they had to get the necessary regulatory approvals required in terms of Egypt's competition law. Finally, in 2012, the two laboratories merged but kept the two separate company names as brands under the new IDH name and management team led by El Sherbini.

This was followed by a listing on the London Stock Exchange in August 2015, making IDH the first Egyptian healthcare company to list in London. Today, the company performs about 26 million tests and services 6.4 million patients annually, and turned a net profit of 384 million Egyptian pounds ($21.4 million) in the 2017 financial year.

GROWTH IN UNSTABLE TIMES

Leading a company through the economic and political uncertainty in North Africa and the Middle East is one thing; doing it in a country where female CEOs are not the norm is another.

In the 2017 *Global Gender Gap Report* published by the World Economic Forum, Egypt ranks 134th out of 144 countries. Since the previous report was published in 2015, the number of women who participate in the labour force has declined to 24.9 per cent compared to 80.4 per cent of men, although the number of female and male tertiary students are almost equal at 35.6 per cent and 36.9 per cent respectively. The report further shows that 85.3 per cent of discouraged job seekers in Egypt are women.

"It is a challenge to be a woman and a leader in our part of the world," El Sherbini admits, and says that overcoming this takes consistency and time. "When you start, there might be people who are not very happy that their boss is a woman but when they see you are serious about what you are doing and that you consistently apply your standards, they accept it."

At IDH, 30 per cent of the employees are women – a ratio they are working to improve. "We don't differentiate at all between women and men, not when it comes to the level of pay or any other area. We completely believe in gender equality," says El Sherbini, and ascribes their current ratio of female to male employees to "the way it is in the countries IDH operates in", as many women start working but leave once they get married or have children.

With every new lab that is established, market research is key. "Since our first expansion drive in 2007, we have continued to do research. Before we branched out into radiology, for example, we actually undertook three research projects. I have always believed in the power of research to focus and develop our strategy," she says.

When looking to expand into new territories or countries, it is often easier to do it by way of acquisitions. That is because,

El Sherbini says, the business will already be established and you can only concentrate on merging the processes and procedures and making sure that management is operating from the same platform and have the same objectives.

"If you are establishing a business from scratch, like the greenfield projects we have done in Sudan, it takes a lot longer. Then you have to get all the approvals, find the location, finish construction, source all the machines, find the people, train them … it could take a year," she explains.

In some cases, regulatory hurdles and red tape have sabotaged growth opportunities. For instance, in Saudi Arabia, they had a partner and a location in place but had to exit due to the restrictions placed on foreign businesses. "There definitely are countries with more difficult regulations, especially for foreigners. Then there are countries that are easier and we are able to work in Jordan, Sudan and now Nigeria," she says.

Yet human resources remain the biggest hurdle. "Finding the right calibre of people, or training the available ones, is definitely a challenge. It is also necessary to motivate our people on an ongoing basis. The people in our part of the world have a lot of capabilities. They are very intelligent and have a lot of talent, but they need to be motivated and put into a system where they can achieve whatever they want. I always tell our employees that the sky is the limit; we, as a team, can achieve anything."

As a leader, she wants to equip and enable IDH's employees to become leaders too. "As we were growing the company, many people who have been with us for a long time needed leadership skills. We require leaders more than managers," she says. Therefore, IDH invests heavily in both technical and soft skills training. It views education as essential for ensuring quality across its branches and brands and has a dedicated training facility with four training laboratories in Cairo. Monthly, the centre provides training to around 100 employees: doctors, chemists, receptionists, branch and area managers, sales personnel and administrators. It also offers new employees, competency-based and needs-based training and practical retraining.

El Sherbini becomes even more serious when the sociopolitical conditions in the region come up. The first few months of 2011, when the Egyptian uprising was at its fiercest, were the most difficult.

"You have to be resilient when facing challenges like that. We had security issues, the banks were closed. There were transport concerns and the attitude of the people changed. I simply tried to focus on what we were really here for and took it day by day," she says. "Sometimes you have to face a force majeure, something you don't really have control over."

On a practical level, it meant having regular human resources and logistics meetings and finding solutions where they could. "We tackled and dealt with problems as they arose. There were problems getting supplies into the country and certain suppliers couldn't deliver. We were keen to solve these problems as quickly as possible to avoid having shortages and not being able to provide a service to our clients."

As a solution, Al Mokhtabar began placing bigger orders. Whereas they normally stock supplies for only two months at their facilities, they ordered large quantities so that they had enough stock and supplies to tide them over if a shipment was delayed.

One year later, when the country was slowly emerging from the unrest and turmoil and the first cabinet under President

Mohamed Morsi was sworn in, the merger with Al Borg materialised. The transaction gave Abraaj an effective 49.9 per cent stake in IDH. Then, in May 2015, Abraaj exited 90 per cent of its stake in IDH through an initial public offering (IPO) on the London Stock Exchange. This was the first ever primary listing of an Egyptian healthcare business in London and the IPO was several times oversubscribed. The IPO share price of $4.45 reflected a market capitalisation of $668 million. Five months later, Abraaj sold its remaining stake in IDH and exited the business entirely.

El Sherbini remembers it as being an extremely busy period which required much hard work but says all the parties cooperated and worked well together. "It was the correct decision at the right time.

"Our main revenue still comes from Egypt, which had a major currency devaluation in 2016. If you translate the company's performance into Egyptian pounds, we have done a very good job," she says. "The investors in IDH are mostly international and they understand that you have to look at the revenues and the impact of forex and do the conversion. We have seen a steady increase in patient volumes and have made some key acquisitions. In 2017, we saw a major drop in purchasing power in Egypt but this is already starting to reverse. People are beginning to invest in the country again and foreign currency is starting to flow back into Egypt."

AT THE HELM OF A MULTINATIONAL

The same thing that initially drove El Sherbini to start the business – to provide a convenient, quality healthcare service that meets high, benchmarked standards – motivates her today.

Her definition of success is simple: to accomplish what you

really want to achieve. For El Sherbini, this was to provide an excellent diagnostic service and a good environment for her employees to work in. "Also, it is is to be able to provide more jobs," she adds.

El Sherbini remains hands-on and manages her staff by setting clear performance indicators and objectives that can be tracked and monitored. After changing from research to clinical pathology, she moved into management when it was required, a journey she continues to relish.

"I enjoy the management part of things. I still do clinical work but not the bench work that came with it. I am actively involved in many of the clinical pathology decisions that our company takes, whether it is how we do new tests or which new areas to move into," she says.

She is passionate about IDH's corporate culture and wants everyone to know that they are part of a family. "They have to know they are influencers and that they are having an impact on people's lives. What we are doing has a direct impact on our patients' lives. Our employees have to know they are doing something incredibly important and that their work makes a difference," she says.

To communicate this and foster a sense of belonging, the management team meets with staff and talks openly about the company results and how their work affects the communities in which they work.

When recounting her own journey, El Sherbini creates the impression that she did not once consider that this road may not work out for her. She is an optimist; not because of a lack of realism, but because she believes it is the only way one can overcome challenges.

"I have received a lot of advice but one piece of advice I have taken to heart came from my father who told me, 'You have to be pragmatic and look at things in a logical way in order to solve any situation'," she says.

Almost surprisingly, she says she believes in luck. "Of course, I believe in luck. It always comes to those people who deserve it, those who work hard and make an effort. I don't think it will come to someone who is not trying."

Being an entrepreneur has changed her and made her wiser. "Some people might see some of the things I have had to do as sacrifices," she says. "I see it as my work. Of course, I have to put in time and effort. There is a balance between work and life but I am not an expert on this. I am trying. As I get older, maybe I am getting better at it."

For the next generation of entrepreneurs in Africa she has this advice: be logical. Dream and be passionate about that dream. Be diligent and show perseverance. It will help you overcome any problem. And always have a conscience and do things the right way.

23.

NJ Ayuk

A lawyer on the road less travelled

By Jaco Maritz

NJ Ayuk's journey didn't follow that of the average student stepping out of an American law school. Instead, he has made a living doing business in countries such as Equatorial Guinea, Angola, South Sudan and the Republic of Congo: places many people will struggle to pinpoint on a map. Ayuk left the well-trodden path to hack open his own way to pursue his ambition of reshaping Africa's natural resources sector. "Yes, I want to make money, but I also want to do something bigger than serving my own personal interests," says the 38-year-old founder and CEO of Centurion Law Group.

From modest beginnings, Ayuk has established himself as a prominent figure in Africa's oil and gas industry. A quick scroll through his LinkedIn posts shows pictures of him shaking hands with Zambian President Edgar Lungu, in the company of the Organisation of the Petroleum Exporting Countries (OPEC) Chairman Mohammed Barkindo in Dubai and meeting with the São Tomé and Príncipe Prime Minister Patrice Trovoada on the sidelines of the football world cup in Russia.

Ayuk has a particular knack for marketing himself. In fact, he considers himself a brand. With close to 200 000 Twitter followers, he is highly active on social media, where he shares his thoughts on business and promotes his speaking engagements. *Big Barrels – African Oil and Gas and the Quest for Prosperity,* his book on the transformative power of the continent's oil industry, appeared in 2017. While traditional members of the legal profession might frown on such self-promotion, Ayuk is unapologetic. "You need to tell your story – if you don't, someone else will tell it, and they are not going to tell it correctly."

SHAPED BY THREE CONTINENTS

Ayuk's early childhood was far removed from his current jet-setting lifestyle. Born in Cameroon, he grew up at the missionary school where his parents were teachers. Due to the country's adverse political and economic situation at the time, his parents thought it best that he complete his high school education in Germany, which they arranged with the help of German missionaries at the school.

"My mother could never turn down an opportunity for education because she knew education would get me out of poverty and allow me to earn more than her $100 salary as a teacher at a missionary school," he says.

At 12, Ayuk went to live with a missionary family in Germany while his parents stayed behind in Cameroon. As a result, he now speaks fluent German. It was there that he found his first paid jobs as a housekeeper at a hotel and working in a fast food restaurant. The German work ethic and focus on efficiency made a lasting impression on him.

Upon finishing secondary school, he was sent to the United States where he became the first member of his family to attend university. He enrolled at the University of Maryland (UMD) in 2000 and graduated with a degree in government and politics.

According to Ayuk, the States played an important role in shaping the person he is today. "I am forever thankful for what America gave me. It showed me that I could come from anything and that I could be anything I wanted to be. America taught me that everybody has a chance – and not only one chance but a second, third and fourth."

At UMD, Ayuk became involved with several organisations which made him aware of the social injustices around him. He worked at the Nyumburu Cultural Centre, which focuses on improving the lives of African-American students, and frequented a nearby Jewish community centre. His studies introduced him to respected African-American lawyers such as Charles Hamilton Houston and Thurgood Marshall, who played important parts in dismantling racial segregation in American schools. His social conscience was further awakened by one of his lecturers, Professor Ronald Walters, who had been campaign manager for Jesse Jackson's two presidential runs. "He always told me, 'You are either going to be a social parasite or a social engineer.'"

Although it was never his plan to become a lawyer, Ayuk began to see it as a profession which would look after him financially while at the same time provide him with a platform to impact society. In 2004, he therefore enrolled at the William Mitchell College of Law.

As a law student, he interned at the United Nations (UN), which he joined full-time after obtaining an MBA from the New York Institute of Technology. He was dispatched to the UN mission in Sudan to provide assistance during the Darfur crisis, an armed conflict that began in 2003 when rebel groups started fighting the government, which they accused of suppressing the non-Arab population in the west of the country. Ayuk was assigned to help with community organisation and governance capacity-building initiatives but became frustrated with the complexity of the situation and the slow pace of change. After a year, he quit.

His time in Sudan, an oil-rich country, made him realise the central role access to natural resources plays in many of Africa's crises. "I learnt that much of Africa's issues are not really about people fighting one another. Much of the continent's crises, wars and problems all come from people wanting a share of their countries' natural resources. I began to see natural resources as ground zero for our survival and our ability to be who we can be.

"I decided if that is the case, I'm going to be part of the solution and get into the industry. I knew nothing about oil and mining. In fact, I hated oil and mining companies. I saw them as the enemy of the people but decided to get in there and find my voice. That was when I knew that I had to get out of the UN and start working in natural resources."

BECOMING AN OIL MAN

Ayuk went to Toronto, Canada, and founded Centurion Law Group, a corporate law and business advisory firm. Since a large number of natural resources companies with operations in Africa are listed on the Toronto Stock Exchange, Ayuk thought he could land business from them. The reality was very different. Ayuk's one-man shop struggled to find solid clients and he had to do small contract jobs to make ends meet. "You've got to eat," he says.

His first big break came in 2009 when a company called

Afex Global wanted to acquire a licence to undertake oil explo-ration in the small Central African country of Equatorial Guinea, which first struck significant oil in the mid-1990s. Before that, the country which has a population of about 860 000, was one the world's poorest nations. Since then major oil producers such as ExxonMobil and Marathon Oil have moved in and its fortunes saw a dramatic turnaround.

Ayuk was asked to review Afex's contract with the Equatoguinean government and make sure it reflected his client's needs. "I had virtually no experience in the oil and gas business and read every freaking thing I could find about the industry to make sure I didn't mess up," he recalls.

"I pushed them to believe I could do it. I was relentless. I was willing to go and live in Equatorial Guinea's capital, Malabo, and work every day to get the deal done. It helped that I was the cheapest; at that stage I didn't really care about the money," Ayuk explains how he, with little experience, managed to land such a relatively important job.

"I knew that if I could get the deal done, bigger things would come," notes Ayuk. And they did. "From that point on, every-thing took off because I came out like the kid who had done a great agreement. The client liked what I did and even the guys on the government side felt they got a good deal."

Centurion slowly established itself as the go-to firm for oil and gas transactions in Equatorial Guinea. When Russian gas giant Gazprom wanted to enter the country, they approached Centurion. However, Ayuk still had to travel to Russia to pitch for the business. "Pitching to Russian businessmen was vastly different. You make jokes and they don't laugh or smile. When I arrived at the airport, they took my passport and looked at it like 50 times. You go in there smiling, thinking you can charm their hearts. It was not the case at all. I had to learn real quick."

Still, he landed the Gazprom contract and helped them to negotiate their entry in Equatorial Guinea. He says respect is the key to any successful negotiation. "The respect you show to the other side can be a dealmaker or a deal-breaker. You should be transparent and tell the other party the truth about your position. If they see that you are trying to pull a fast one, everything you do becomes suspicious. Over the years I've negotiated with warlords and hostage takers, people who make you want to go to the bathroom to wash your hands with sanitiser after you've shaken their hands. Still, we've been able to get the deals done by being respectful."

An oil exploration company called Vanco, now PanAtlantic, offered Ayuk the opportunity to become country manager of its unit in Equatorial Guinea. He said yes, on condition that he could continue to run Centurion. "I let them know that I was going to keep my law firm. I wasn't going to kill it. The agreement worked out well. I did the work, everybody was happy, I didn't miss a report, I didn't miss a thing."

His 18 months at Vanco was a crash course in management, interacting with government and dealing with suppliers. The job also gave him insight into the way oil companies think and how governments often shoot themselves in the foot when negotiating oil contracts. "It was like being a prosecutor who had to become a defence attorney. I kept going to meetings with governments and kept seeing how they messed up. I saw their shortcomings and how they entered negotiations without being prepared. As an African sitting on the other side, this really upset me."

EXPANDING HIS HORIZONS

Centurion now represents Equatorial Guinea's Ministry of Mines and Hydrocarbons and negotiates oil contracts on the government's behalf. Ayuk is frequently seen with the Minister, Gabriel Mbaga Obiang Lima, who is popular with foreign investors and considered a capable operator among politicians who tend to make headlines for the wrong reasons.

Their initial meeting was a case of being in the right place at the right time. Ayuk attended an oil and gas conference in London where Obiang Lima, then Equatorial Guinea's Vice Minister of Petroleum, spoke passionately about increasing local companies' participation in the oil industry and revealed plans to develop the country's natural gas industry. Ayuk was impressed but wasn't able to speak to the Minister at the conference. However, as luck would have it, as he was travelling from the airport building to his plane, the Minister stepped onto the bus.

"We had a quick chat and I told him about my work. He said, 'Listen, when you get to Malabo tomorrow, come to my office.' He assigned me to work with one of his people. I didn't have a contract and I didn't know if I was going to get paid but the work was great. I felt this is me – I'm in a position to take on these multinational oil companies that I believe had been screwing our people."

As he wasn't representing any major oil companies at the time, working for the government didn't present a conflict of interest. Centurion's clients were mostly service providers to the industry for whom the firm handled matters such as employment contracts and service agreements.

Now that he had a solid base in Equatorial Guinea, Ayuk

could expand Centurion's presence to countries such as Ghana, Cameroon and South Africa. It also has affiliates in the Republic of the Congo and South Sudan.

Ayuk works round the clock and is constantly taking calls and sending emails from his multiple phones. He expects the same dedication from his employees and concedes that he is a hard taskmaster. "We work from Monday to Sunday. I'm very demanding, but I don't ask my team to do what I wouldn't do myself.

"You've got to motivate your staff and pay them well. You've got to encourage them and you've got to let them know there is a big future, which they need to see in front of everything they do." But he warns against holding on to toxic employees. "You should never have people on your team who are cancerous. Cut them loose, even though it hurts. There is never a good time to fire someone. When employees start being negative, you have to let them go, no matter how good they are."

Dealing with clients from all over the world also brings challenges. For instance, in the Middle East the work week starts on a Sunday, which is generally a day off in most African countries. Ayuk turned this into a competitive advantage by being available on a Sunday. "My Middle Eastern clients now say, 'I'm down with NJ because the Centurion guys are going to respond to me on a Sunday.'"

GIVING AFRICA A SEAT AT THE TABLE

Ayuk was actively involved in lobbying for Equatorial Guinea's admittance to OPEC, one of the world's most powerful organisations, in 2017. By increasing or decreasing oil supply, OPEC member states wield enormous influence on the oil price, which determines what people around the world pay to fill up their tanks. He believes African oil producers shouldn't be sitting on the sidelines of global decision-making in the oil industry, and Centurion has subsequently also successfully advocated for the Republic of the Congo's admission to OPEC in 2018.

Being allowed into OPEC is no mean feat. "They don't give you a rulebook. You have to figure it out. I was lucky that I had a contact who introduced me to the right people, whereafter I used my networks. When you reach that point, your network is your net worth. After you've made your case to the OPEC oil ministers, they gather in a room and discuss your application while you wait in a separate area until they've reached their decision. It's like electing the Pope."

Ayuk admits it was "scary" to deal with such powerful people, but says that David took on Goliath even though he knew he was a big giant. "He beat him because he felt a sense of duty. Assuring Africa of a voice at the table will have far-reaching implications."

The bulk of Centurion's clients are directly or indirectly involved in the oil industry. In the first few years after 2010 when Brent Crude traded well above $100 a barrel, those in the oil sector were printing money. Then, in 2014, it all came crashing down and the price hit a low of under $30 a barrel at the beginning of 2016. Ayuk says this was a tough time: "Everyone, including me, took a blow. I had to let people go and ask some employees to take a salary cut."

While many believe that the oil industry's very existence is challenged by electric vehicles, Ayuk is not too worried. He is especially bullish on natural gas, which is found in close proximity to oil deposits. Natural gas power plants are becoming increasingly popular, he says, as they are cheaper and more environmentally friendly than coal alternatives. "The future is gas. You need gas to power electric vehicles. Solar or wind energy is not going to take over anytime soon. The petroleum value chain will still be necessary."

Much of Africa's oil deposits are in countries with questionable governance and human rights records, but for Ayuk, it's a matter of looking further than the here and now. "I'm not doing what I do for the government, I'm doing it for the state. There is a difference between government and state. The state will continue but governments come and go. You are creating a legacy for that country because those who come later will pick it up and hopefully do the right things, even though the right things are not always being done at the moment. You have to think about the future.

"I'm prepared to work where people don't want to go. Some of the best deals we've done have been in difficult, tough places. I'm doing deals in places like South Sudan, Somalia, Angola and the Niger Delta in Nigeria. Sometimes you have to follow the road less travelled."

24.

Polo Leteka

The investor who spots opportunity where others see risk

By Glenneis Kriel

South African entrepreneur Polo Leteka makes it her business to bridge the gap between small to medium-sized enterprises (SMEs) and investors. In 2008, she co-founded investment company IDF Capital, which at the time raised funding mainly to invest in black female entrepreneurs. Concentrating on this group of entrepreneurs made sense to her because black female business owners had been overlooked and put at a disadvantage even after the country had become a democracy in 1994.

A decade later, IDF Capital manages investment funds for institutional as well as corporate investors. Their institutional investors, which include South Africa's Industrial Development Corporation and the Small Enterprise Finance Agency, have a mandate to invest in SMEs and black- and female-owned businesses. The corporate investors, such as Shell, chemicals group AECI, telecoms operator Telkom and rail transport company Gibela, are required to invest in black-owned SMEs to meet the Enterprise and Supplier Development (ESD) requirements of South Africa's Broad-Based Black Economic Empowerment (BBBEE) codes of good practice.

BBBEE is a government initiative aimed at distributing wealth to those who were discriminated against by the apartheid system. Companies are required to be BBBEE compliant if they want to do business with state-owned entities and to be seen as good corporate citizens.

While institutions and companies want to reach their transformation targets, they also want to get good returns on their investments. "Our funds are structured according to the private equity fund model and the principles are similar. What differs are the types and quantum of returns required. In our case, there is great emphasis on social impact and some form of commercial return and, in some cases, capital preservation, depending on the investor," Leteka says.

IDF Capital makes money from management fees (a percentage of the fund size) and also participates in any returns over and above what is promised to investors. The bulk of IDF Capital's clients are institutional investors and Leteka's primary task is to keep them happy. Their offices are, for example, situated in Sandton in Johannesburg to be close to their biggest clients. "Dealing with investors at this level requires a certain type of sophistication and you cannot work from home. You need formal, professional offices," she says.

As their competition grew, the business expanded its scope by establishing subsidiary companies that offer more focused services. In 2015, IDF Capital ventured into West Africa with Alitheia IDF, a company co-founded with Alitheia Capital in Lagos, Nigeria.

Leteka's companies now manage a total of R650 million ($44 million) in investment funds and employ a staff of 35. Between 2008 and 2018, they have invested in excess of 150 entrepreneurs, thousands of business owners have undergone their training programmes and around 40 start-ups have participated in the I'M IN pre-investment accelerator programme since its launch in 2017.

IDENTIFYING A BUSINESS OPPORTUNITY

Leteka was born in Lesotho and grew up in Mahikeng, about 300km west of Johannesburg, in a family with a strong entrepreneurial spirit. Several of her aunts, uncles, cousins and siblings have their own businesses, which include an engineering consultancy, a laundromat, a catering company, an interior design company, a shop and a childcare business. They not only made her want to run her own business, but gave her a realistic glimpse of the hardship and challenges an entrepreneur often has to deal with.

After school, she obtained a BCom followed by an honours degree in accounting through the University of South Africa (Unisa) and a post graduate diploma in auditing at the University of Johannesburg. Her accounting background has made her comfortable with numbers which, she says, is a prerequisite for a successful business.

"Many people are intimidated by the numbers side of business, but I see it as a story that tells you whether the business is moving backward or forward. It tells you whether you are making good decisions, whether you are selling enough products to cover your costs, whether your products are priced correctly and your workers are earning their salaries, or whether money is wasted on certain inputs," Leteka explains.

Besides her studies, she gained valuable experience working in the private and public sector from 1997 to 2007. First, she did her articles at Gobodo Incorporated, now SNG Grant Thornton, before learning about investment banking, public-policy formulation, venture capital and private equity during her time with AloeCap, an investment and financial-services company.

She then joined the South African Department of Trade and Industry, where she realised the extent of the barriers to entry for SMEs while leading the team that developed the first BBBEE codes of good practice designed to accelerate black economic empowerment in the private sector.

"I realised the problem was not a lack of capital, as everyone tends to believe, but the risk aversion of banks. There is a lot of money lying around to invest in businesses but most of it is reserved for businesses with low risks, not new entrepreneurs and start-ups with no track record," she explains.

Leteka saw this as a business opportunity and, in 2008, along with her then business partner, launched IDF Capital (known as IDF Managers at the time). "My research revealed a gap in the market for a middleman, someone who on the one hand can help the small to medium-sized entrepreneur to better articulate their value proposition to investors and, on the other hand, make investing in such businesses more attractive to financial institutions."

The company was launched with the help of start-up funding from Anglo Zimele, an Anglo American enterprise development fund that helps historically disadvantaged South Africans to own and run businesses. Thanks to her existing network in the industry, Leteka could research the market thoroughly and build a convincing case for her business.

"Viable businesses are built on creative solutions. The trick is to dig deep to understand whether the problem you're trying to solve is as big as you think it is and to see what solutions others have come up with, so that you can determine if your solution is better than what is already available.

"You have to think carefully about the other players and what you will bring that would give you a competitive edge. You also have to determine if your solution will be financially viable; in other words, whether people will be willing to pay for it," Leteka says.

Relatively little was known about black-women-owned SMEs when Leteka and her team began IDF Capital. They rigorously studied as much as they could but learnt "thousands of things" more by talking to the women they were targeting. Reading academic papers and googling is one thing, Leteka says, but you have to talk to people and hear first-hand what their needs are.

ON-THE-JOB TRAINING

Leteka left a good job to found a high-risk business. "Even after the company was up and running, I was sometimes tempted to take up one of the high-paying job offers that still came my way. But I never did. I was set on realising my dream," she says.

During the first few years, institutional investors were not coming to the party as quickly as she had anticipated and things became stressful. "Our biggest barrier was to convince them to commit capital to invest in businesses that everyone wanted to run away from at the time. It was a terribly difficult and taxing task and we had many rejections," she recalls.

To make ends meet, she was forced to sell her properties, including the house she had been living in. "I've been buying property since I was 24 and having to live in a rented house was particularly hard for me. I have only been able to buy my own house again this year."

At one point Leteka was so disillusioned about their financial situation that she told her business partner they would have to close down if they did not secure funding by the end of the month. Fortunately, an institutional investor made a capital commitment to their fund, which helped them to get back on track. "That contract was the tipping point. It is scary to think I would have called it a day if that capital commitment had come a couple of weeks later," she says.

"People think it is great being your own boss and that you are the boss of your own time, but the truth is entrepreneurs generally have to work much harder than salaried people. Their whole future depends on the success of their business and you end up eating, sleeping and drinking work. You don't have as much time as you would have liked to spend with family, friends, hobbies or leisure. You need to have a partner who understands this and supports you, otherwise they will become an added drain on your energies."

IDF Capital was not Leteka's first business. She had started a bed and breakfast in Mahikeng when she was 28 years old and working full-time in Pretoria. "My job required me to be on the road quite a lot and I got the idea to start a bed and breakfast when I visited one with quite a homey vibe," she says. It lasted only two years. "It turned out that a bed and breakfast was a lifestyle business that requires the owner to be there all the time. Because I was 300km away and because my mom and cousin, who managed it on my behalf, neither shared my vision nor had any of the required skills to make the business work, it turned into a complete failure."

The biggest lesson she learnt from this early failure is to first of all do thorough homework before embarking on a new venture. This entails identifying the opportunities, risks and threats as well as ways to alleviate and leverage them, drawing up a business plan and planning for the future.

She also learnt the importance of attracting top staff and creating innovative ways to keep them. "At IDF we made the mistake of appointing the people we could afford instead of those we really wanted and needed. You have to get the best if you want to be the best in your field. To overcome this, we initiated creative ways to compensate employees for their expertise by, for example, offering them shares and great career prospects. Because of this, some of our first employees are now owners in our businesses."

They also take great care to recruit staff with good entrepreneurial skills and who share Leteka's business vision. "I have gone to great lengths to institutionalise a culture of open communication where everyone is encouraged to think for themselves and is free to share their ideas and opinions. More heads are always better than one. It helps you to make better-informed decisions."

While employees are given freedom when it comes to taking decisions, Leteka always takes full and final responsibility in those areas that are critical to the success of the company, such as relations with investors and regulatory compliance.

This wasn't always the case and the company's licence was suspended because it did not comply with all the necessary regulations. All operations were put on hold until the matter was sorted out. Now Leteka knows better. "The incident taught me to keep my eye on the ball. You cannot leave important matters to chance and have to take the final responsibility for them."

Planning for growth has been one of the greatest challenges

and is something she sees many companies struggle with. "The problem is that you cannot duplicate what you have done to start a R1-million business to turn it into a R10-million business. For that type of expansion, a whole new plan, systems and team might be necessary. It's also important not to dilute the company culture while growing the business, as this is an integral driver of a company's success," she says.

Leteka believes having a business partner is an advantage, since partners bring different knowledge, skills and strengths to the table that enhance the overall business offering. Partners also serve as sounding boards and provide support during difficult times, which is essential because being an entrepreneur can be "quite a lonely journey".

NURTURING SMALL BUSINESSES

The SMEs in which IDF invests are mainly found through word of mouth or are referred by its investors and business associates. Among the ones Leteka is particularly proud of are The Mediwell Group and Mhlavazi.

Mediwell was started by two black female doctors who were seeking start-up funding for a medical centre. "We appointed a business support service provider to guide them along their entrepreneurial journey and played a big role in legal negotiations with some of their service providers," she says.

Mhlavazi is a retail strip in Limpopo province built on tribal land in a rural area. The proprietor initially used his pension money to start building it but ran out midway through the development. "We had to negotiate with the tribal authority to recognise our rights as funders to the strip even though it was on their land, and to mitigate the risk that we might not be able to recover our money should the tribal authority exercise its ownership rights to the land. We also assisted with negotiations with anchor tenants to secure decent rentals," she says. Where the people in the area previously had to travel long distances to do their shopping, they now have access to all the main banks and stores such as Pep and Shoprite.

Leteka was one of the judges, or "dragons", on the first season of South Africa's *Dragons' Den*, a television programme where entrepreneurs pitch their business ideas to investors. While the dragons are portrayed as having bottomless pools of money, Leteka says those investment decisions were made cautiously.

"I was not using my own money on the show but IDF Capital's and we had strict rules as to how the money could be spent and on what. Entrepreneurs had to comply with several criteria to qualify. We identified five possible investments on television but upon close inspection and after doing due diligence, we invested in only three businesses," she says.

The television show made her more aware of the problems that new entrepreneurs are experiencing, which led her and her fellow dragons to co-author *And For All These Reasons, I'm In* in which they tell of their own journeys as entrepreneurs, including the highlights and lowlights. The book led them to establish the I'M IN accelerator programme to help prepare entrepreneurs seeking investment.

For now, Leteka is focusing on growing the business in South Africa and expanding further into the African continent. "The issues which are preventing entrepreneurs from growing in South Africa are similar to the ones found in the rest of Africa. It makes sense to use the great insights and business experience we have gained here to solve problems in other African countries."

Moving beyond South Africa comes with its own risks and Leteka is managing them by forming partnerships, like Alitheia IDF in Nigeria, in each country. "It is very important to have a local partner when you enter a new country, as they bring essential insights into the business environment and culture of that country."

Even though she is still in her forties, Leteka hopes that the company will become self-sufficient so that she will be able to "retire". "I am investing a lot of time and energy in this company. Ten years from now I would like to downscale and rather focus on more socially responsible projects and giving back to the community. I am still doing some policy consulting on the side, and would also like to spend more time on this."

25.

Ashley Uys
Diagnostic hustler

By Jeanette Clark

Ashley Uys is not a born entrepreneur.

If asked, he would say that he doesn't believe that some people are born with the ability to be entrepreneurs and others aren't. "I believe that an entrepreneur can be developed," he says. "There are dormant or latent entrepreneurs out there who just need a spark to blossom."

That's most likely because he himself became an entrepreneur out of frustration. Out of necessity. He took charge of his own destiny because of an immense sense of responsibility and of wanting to get out of his circumstances.

Uys, 36, has been lauded as one of Africa's rising young businessmen. He established his first company at the age of 24 and has since added two more successful medical technology ventures that offer solutions to communities in crisis with low-cost diagnostic tests.

When interviewed for the *21 Icons* series, this South African biotechnologist and innovator tells how, when a bursary allowed him to go to university, he'd see students sitting around and enjoying *braais* (a South African pastime of cooking meat on an open fire), and would think: "You are here with your mother's money and you are having a *braai*? Why are you not working?"

He is the eldest of six children, a position he readily admits came with its own challenges. Most of his childhood was spent in Bishop Lavis on the Cape Flats, an area outside Cape Town in South Africa where gangsterism is rife.

When he speaks of this time, there is a quiet resolve and determination in his voice. He was never satisfied with the hand life dealt him and vowed to make it different – for himself and for his family.

"My biggest motivation was to make a success of my life. One of the things that I remember growing up was not having the things other kids had, such as shoes, fancy clothes. It frustrated me. I realised that I would sacrifice a lot of time and energy to make sure that I got myself out of those circumstances," he says.

Uys's father contributed hugely to his sense of self-belief. "When I was about five years old, my dad motivated me to do things that went beyond what is normally expected of a five-year-old. He helped me and made me read newspapers. He made me believe our circumstances were temporary. He even taught me how to use power tools. It made me feel older, stronger, than I actually was."

During school holidays, his father took him along to the construction sites where he had worked and let Uys work there for extra money. With his savings, Uys bought a welder and grinder, so he could make gates and burglar bars.

When Uys was 15, his father lost his construction contract. At that stage his mother was unemployed too. "It was tough. Family members had to bring us food. It frustrated me. I made flyers and gave them out to neighbours and other members of the community to advertise my welding service. A friend and I walked around the whole day. We got one job but when we arrived at the house the owner said we were too young."

Sport helped to keep him motivated. He also worked hard on biology and physical science, which he enjoyed. His sacrifices and putting in the time to study earned him a bursary for under-graduate studies in biotechnology at the University of the West-ern Cape (UWC). Upon graduating, he received a scholarship to study towards an honours degree in biotechnology before being offered a scarce skills scholarship for a master's degree.

TRADING ACADEMIA FOR THE REAL WORLD

"I wanted to be in this industry and manufacture products by using my science skills. I didn't ever just want to be a researcher or an academic. I didn't just want to be in a job, earning a salary – overqualified and stuck."

For this reason, he declined the master's scholarship and found a job at the University of Cape Town where he did genetic research and mapped the HIV virus and its different strains. "Although I was receiving a salary, I was still doing research for publication purposes, for research's sake. I was still doing the same thing I was doing at university and it was not where I wanted to be."

It was then that he was accepted into a business incubator programme that offered internships for scientists from univer-sities. Uys was one of 13 shortlisted candidates and it was a turning point for him.

The course load was equivalent to half an MBA and taught him the theory of marketing, business administration and finan-cial management. To pass the internship, funded by the Depart-ment of Science and Technology, candidates had to write a business plan for their host companies, or for their own business. Uys was the only one among the 13 to write a plan for starting his own company. He made a deal with his host employer so he could still work for them for three days a week, establishing Real World Diagnostics at the same time to produce diagnostic test kits. At 24, Uys officially became a CEO.

FACING THE CHALLENGES HEAD-ON

While chatting to Uys, it quickly becomes clear he has a self-awareness that came through tough life lessons. He puts almost as much stock in the failures along his business journey as in his successes.

And there definitely were failures and mistakes.

For one whole year, Real World Diagnostics didn't make a single sale. His business partner (who owned 30 per cent of the business) opted out because it had become too tough; he gave back his shares and moved on.

Uys found himself up against a wall. It was make-or-break time. His business ingenuity kicked in and he began looking for an opportunity. He hustled. This would become a theme throughout the initial growth period of his companies – find a gap, make a plan, negotiate and leverage.

He saw a rapid diagnostic testing kit for methamphetamine (or *tik*, which is a widely used illegal drug on the Cape Flats) from a supplier in the United States and looked for a way to import and distribute it in South Africa. While negotiating with the supplier to get sample kits, Uys approached Alpha Pharm, the largest national group of independent community pharmacies in South Africa.

"I begged them for a meeting," he says. "They eventually gave me 10 minutes during the lunch break at one of their management meetings in Cape Town. I knew my elevator pitch had to be way up there."

Uys spent the 10 minutes talking about his childhood. He showed them before and after pictures of drug users. He understood his target audience and spoke to their objectives. Ultimately, he pitched the product as a corporate social responsibility initiative for the company, knowing the tax incentive they would receive would count in his favour.

Alpha Pharm awarded him the national contract to distribute the kit. Once he had that, Uys could negotiate better repayment terms over a longer period with the supplier in the United States. "I basically bootstrapped a model where I didn't need big funding to start the business."

Using Alpha Pharm as a reference and leverage, he signed up another wholesaler and started importing a second product, this time a pregnancy test. "I could then tell this supplier: 'Guys, I can move volume here.' It was simply a case of attracting one party and getting the contract to be able to negotiate with others. This was how I was going to survive. Wheeling and dealing is part of life on the Cape Flats. I've always said the gangsters there would make great businessmen."

The money he made this way allowed him to build his business until he had the capital to consider manufacturing the products in South Africa. "I first went back to the university where I had worked and asked for lab space. The head of the department, who I knew, agreed to let me use lab space for free if I brought some of my own equipment."

This allowed him to develop two diagnostic tests – a malaria test and a drug test – that outperformed the ones already on the market in terms of specificity and accuracy. Just then, one of his clients was looking for a malaria test and Uys struck a deal with them: they would buy the necessary raw materials on his behalf and he would simply deduct the cost from the price of the final product. Thus he overcame his cash flow problem to scale up manufacturing.

Finally, he was able to rent factory space in Muizenberg outside Cape Town and in 18 months he manufactured close to two million units. "I made enough capital to reinvest in the facility. Over time the clientele grew."

It also allowed him to appoint his first employee, years after establishing Real World Diagnostics. The number of employees has since grown to 40 in total across his three companies: Real World Diagnostics, Medical Diagnostech (established in 2010) and OculusID (in 2013). Medical Diagnostech expanded on the original Real World Diagnostics' product range, while OculusID uses image capturing and processing technology to evaluate pupil response and thus detect impairment in individuals due to substance abuse, physiological defects or fatigue.

Uys has always found a way to achieve what he wanted – whether it was leveraging the Alpha Pharm name to obtain favourable payment terms with an overseas supplier or convincing his internship host company to keep him on three days a week while he was establishing his own business.

But there was a moment when Uys thought he would lose it all. He remembers the day clearly when the sheriff of the court came to his home to write up his assets. It was a difficult and dark moment, when everything he had worked towards could have been lost.

Uys was approached by a third party to find a solution for a client abroad. A German company needed a diagnostic test which could establish whether someone had consumed any alcohol in the last 48 hours to be used at rehabilitation clinics.

Within a short time, he produced a prototype and signed a contract with the third party without first handing it to legal representatives to check. This led to a dispute between the third party and Uys about the payments due and who the intellectual property for the solution resided with. The case ended up in court and legal costs began stacking up. When Uys lost the case, the other party's legal costs became his responsibility too.

He now speaks with wry self-deprecation about his biggest mistake but there is still some bite in his voice. "Don't be a know-it-all. Give contracts to lawyers to check out. I had to learn to know my strengths and weaknesses and to be calm and negotiate properly."

Once again he hustled. He knew one of the components in his tests was more sensitive than what was available in the market. He sent a sample to a company in France, offering to sell it to them for €100 000 ($116 000). "I still remember playing indoor cricket with friends and having to go to the ATM to draw money. That's when I saw more than R1 million in my account and realised they had paid me for it. I used the money to settle my outstanding legal bills."

In other words, he got lucky.

Uys disagrees.

MAKING HIS OWN LUCK

"Luck – you bring it about yourself. If you have a plan A, plan B, plan C – then plan A is very lucky; plan B is just lucky; plan C is satisfying. If you have a network and you've built resources to the point where you know it is significant, you will have more luck. You will have several plans to fall back on."

He does believe in the power and importance of having strong mentors, though. First, there was his father. Then, at the UWC, he encountered Clifford Jacobs, who still works at the university as a senior scientific officer. Jacobs challenged Uys during his studies, when his short-lived dream was to become a forensic scientist. "He told me, 'You are one of the smartest guys in this class, why do you want to go into that field? Because you like *Medical Detectives* and *CSI* on television?' He encouraged me to go into biotechnology instead, to do something that was going to boost the industry."

Another of his UWC lecturers played a pivotal role, not only by motivating Uys to perform at his best academically, but in shaping the underlying culture at his businesses. Professor Sean Davison, who later attracted much attention for assisting his terminally ill mother to end her life, was already controversial in his approaches at the university. Uys tells how Davison put up a reward with his own money to incentivise students during exams. The best student took home the cash reward.

Today, at Medical Diagnostech, employees are rewarded for their hard work and for adding value. "Every year, no matter how the company performed, we have a proper staff party and bonus payouts. Whoever adds value, gets an on-the-spot bonus," Uys says.

He is honest about the fact that he does not really see himself as a CEO. "My passion is not running an operation. My motivation is to become a significant player in the industry and my drive is innovation. I actually dislike the manufacturing part," he admits readily. "Ideally I would like to innovate and then find the right people to run the companies."

On the horizon is a new venture, this time quite far removed from the fields in which he has played with his diagnostic kits. This new opportunity in the beauty industry has come about by coincidence. The Medical Diagnostech team works with gold nanoparticles as a product of the reduction process they conduct in the lab when producing the diagnostic tests. The surface charge of these nanoparticles is negative. Uys and his team have found a way to utilise these nanoparticles to achieve the effects of sought-after beauty regimes such as Brazilian hair treatments in a fraction of the time.

"We are busy with the business model at this moment and have already seen interest from the industry. We are going to take it to market soon," he relays with excitement about this new opportunity.

You can immediately tell when Uys believes there is a breakthrough or a possibility that lies ahead. His tone becomes urgent, excited and animated. It is also the tone and pace he uses when speaking about the possibilities in Africa, its people and the untapped potential contained in the challenges facing the continent.

The development of people and particularly mentoring young people are priorities for him. He exposes his employees to training courses and education opportunities to develop the skills they need to help build the companies to the next level. He is constantly looking for ways to promote those who add value to the business and is in favour of providing equity and ownership opportunities to those with entrepreneurial potential.

"At UWC we had brilliant mentors who played a big part in building me as a person. That is why I dedicate my time going back to the university. I have interns from there working for me at the moment," he says of his role now that he has become the mentor. "Job creation is still a big part of the drive behind what I do. To see heads of households come and find employment. There is worth and value in that."

One of the things he is proudest of is the fact that he could employ his entire family to make sure none of them will again find themselves in the circumstances that once frustrated him so.

Uys has hustled himself into a new life.

Made in the USA
Columbia, SC
27 May 2020